Lisa MURPHY on
PLAY

Other Redleaf Press Books by Lisa Murphy

The Ooey Gooey® Handbook
Ooey Gooey® Tooey
Even More Fizzle, Bubble, Pop & Wow!

Lisa Murphy on play

The foundation of children's learning

Lisa Murphy

Redleaf Press®
www.redleafpress.org
800-423-8309

Published by Redleaf Press
10 Yorkton Court
St. Paul, MN 55117
www.redleafpress.org

First edition published 2009. Second edition 2016
Cover design by Amy Fastenau
Cover photographs/illustrations by Yarruta
Interior design by Amy Fastenau
Typeset in PMN Caecilia and Lemon Sans
Printed in the United States of America

Library of Congress Cataloging-in-Publication Data
Names: Murphy, Lisa, 1969- author.
Title: Lisa Murphy on play : the foundation of children's learning / Lisa
    Murphy.
Other titles: Play-- the foundation that supports the house of higher
    learning | Play
Description: Second edition. | St. Paul, MN : Redleaf Press, [2016] | Earlier
    edition published as: Play-- the foundation that supports the house of
    higher learning. | Includes bibliographical references.
Identifiers: LCCN 2015040240 | ISBN 9781605544410 (pbk.) | ISBN 9781605544427
    (ebook)
Subjects: LCSH: Play. | Early childhood education. | Child development.
Classification: LCC HQ782 .M866 2016 | DDC 155.4/18--dc23
LC record available at http://lccn.loc.gov/2015040240

Printed on acid-free paper

U16-08

For my brother Tom.

I had something to say—you helped me say it.

*Necessity may be the mother of invention,
but play is most certainly the father.*

Roger von Oech, *A Whack on the Side of the Head*

Contents

Introduction to the Second Edition

WHEN I WROTE the first edition of *Play*, I wanted to capture the essence of where I was in my career. David Heath at Redleaf Press said it read as though I had a point to make, something to prove. And he was right. I joked that I wanted every line to have a reference or footnote in an effort to show readers that play-based early childhood programming wasn't Lisa Murphy's *personal preference*, but is actually what is supported in the research.

Since *Play* was initially published, my theories and patience have been challenged and tested. This led to both a broadening and deepening of my understanding of early childhood education. In addition, my desire to *prove* has evolved more into a commitment to *connecting*. What does that mean? To put it plainly, I have ceased defending that which has already been proven. Instead of spending energy on feeble efforts to *prove* (which often fall on deaf, stubborn ears), I put this same energy into connecting people with the evidence. How do I do this? I put the burden of proof on the naysayer. What does *that* mean? It means if you tell me I need to eliminate recess, do flash cards with preschoolers, or do the calendar with toddlers, I am going to professionally respond, "What page is that on?" or "Where is that supported in the research?" or "Why?" or "Prove it."

THE Binder CHaLLenge

The reason I can push back with confidence is because I hold myself accountable to the same challenge I currently propose to my workshop audience members, social media followers, and readers. What is that challenge, you ask? It is the Binder Challenge. I have outlined it in detail in other places, but in a nutshell, and for the sake of page counts and time, this is what you do:

1. Get a binder.

2. On the front write PLAYFUL LEARNING = SCHOOL READINESS with subtitle PRESENTING THE EVIDENCE.

3. Then, from this point forward every time you find something that supports a hands-on, play-based, relationship-based, child-centered, developmentally appropriate, early childhood environment, you copy it and put it in your binder. It might be any of the following:

   - an article
   - a letter to an editor
   - a photograph you took of a playful sign at a playground
   - a book (But don't copy the book! That's ILLEGAL! Copy the cover and the copyright page.)
   - workshop notes
   - workshop handouts
   - playful activity ideas/recipes
   - blog posts
   - links to various playful websites
   - research studies
   - scholarly papers that you or someone else wrote

Anything that reinforces and supports the fact that this mind-set and approach **is not new** goes in your binder. Anything that reminds naysayers that this is not simply our personal preference now goes in your binder. Anything that supports the fact that this is not just what we "like" or what we "want" but is in actuality supported by the literature, data, science, and experience now gets read, copied, and put it in your binder.

4. When someone comes to the school, your room, the office, your family child care, the playroom, wherever and is like, "PPPLLLLLLLLLAAAAYYYY? YOU STILL PLAY? OMG! THEY ARE GOING TO KINDERGARTEN IN THREE YEARS! HOW CAN YOU DO THIS?"

You take a big, deep, loving breath [this part—the love part—is *way* more important than you might realize!] and say, "Yes. Playful learning [this is important, say it all together, 'playful learning'] leads to, supports, increases [pick something that works for your mouth] school readiness. And *this* [point to kids engaged] is what it looks like! And *this* [point to the binders] is what supports it.

[pause] "May I make you a cup of coffee?"

On a more personal note, quite a bit has happened since I originally published *Play*. I earned my M.Ed. in early childhood education, began some fruitful collaborative projects with many other passionate play-based educators, and watched this book evolve from an idea to being printed to being a popular book club suggestion to being a college textbook to being an e-book! I have had the fortunate opportunity to present workshops in almost every U.S. state, Jamaica, and most of Canada (including the Arctic Circle!), and signed on with Redleaf Press as one of their authors. I am proud to be working with them on this updated edition and am grateful for their input on the process.

I had been toying around with whether *Play* needed a revision, and every time I reread it, I'll be honest with you, I said to myself, "No, leave it alone." Why? Because while, in formal academic-speak, in research years it is approaching being "dated," the core message is the same, still accurate and on point. So I left it alone. Then it came to my attention that the fifth edition of the *Diagnostic and Statistical Manual of Mental Disorders* (DSM-5) was going to be published in 2013. The DSM lists the diagnostic criteria for psychological disorders.

The fifth edition was to contain many changes, including modifications to how attention deficit disorder (ADD) and attention deficit/hyperactivity disorder (ADHD) were categorized. (For the curious, they are no longer two separate diagnoses; the term used now is ADHD.)

The proposed changes to the language used in the DSM-5 are what really pushed me to consider an update to Play, as I didn't want new readers referencing outdated information from chapter 2 (MOVE) of the book. Initially I planned on only revising this one chapter. But a handful of colleagues who remain infinitely more insightful than myself persuaded me to reconsider by telling me that there was a good chance that my writing voice and my knowledge base had changed since the original publication. "Why infuse only one part of the book with this?" they asked. "It might sound choppy and inconsistent," they said. True words, honest words, complimentary words, yet all my brain heard was THAT WILL TAKE MORE TIME! ALERT! ALERT! THAT WILL MAKE MORE WORK! RESIST! RESIST!

But in the end I knew they were right. So we changed the title, made a plan for revising the guts, slapped a new picture on the cover, and gave the whole book a trip to the editorial day spa. Why put in the effort? Because a child's right to play continues to come under attack, and this is no longer acceptable. Our culture continues to reinforce the false dichotomy of playing versus learning, incorrectly believing that when children play they are being deprived of something more important.

I am not, am **NOT**, going to stop being developmentally appropriate, nor will I second-guess best practice because the person in front of me has never seen it! And I will NOT compromise the childhood experience just because the school down the street, which might charge $20 less a week, does! Nor will I cease doing what is right and best for the kids just because the teacher down the hall is inconvenienced by it!

Now, don't get fired because you are reading this book! But it is important to realize that there is no need to reinvent the wheel. The framework of what constitutes "developmentally appropriate" exists. The research that supports playful learning exists. The anecdotes exist. The success stories exist. Why some early childhood people continue to resist embracing play, even in the face of decades of research that supports it, boggles the mind. We know better yet continue to be faced with this huge disconnect between theory and practice. Which is a fancy way of saying that we know better yet for some reason aren't willing to act on it.

I selfishly hope that something in this book might assist you in taking a baby step toward reinfusing play in the lives of young children; perhaps a particular story or data point might increase your confidence as you speak out with me as an advocate of playful learning. I do not claim to have all the answers, and what I offer here represents only the tip of the iceberg of available evidence that supports the cause of play. That being said, it is with unbridled passion, outspoken advocacy, and a spirit of sharing that I offer the contents contained herein as resources, stories, evidence, and information that might assist us in our combined efforts to show that play is the foundation of children's learning.

PART 1

HOW I GOT HERE

1

Mornings with Mary

SHE OPENED THE door and stepped out onto the porch. She was Miss Mary. My new teacher, my first teacher. She smiled as I scampered up the walkway and up the steps to the front door. She bent down, looked me right in the eye, took my hand, and said, "Come on in, let me show you what we do here."

I was three years old, and this was my first day of school. Mary proceeded to take me on a tour of the little house that was Mary's Nursery School. This is what I remember: The first room was filled with wooden unit blocks, Legos, cars, carpet squares, dollhouses, and huge hollow blocks. Over the years, hundreds of children spent hours in this room designing, balancing, measuring, and engineering the architectural feats of childhood. You could stay in this room until you were done. Absent were adults flicking lights, singing cute songs, and making us clean up before we were finished.

Mary and I walked into the second room. If we viewed that room today, through a Reggio lens, it would now be referred to as the atelier. It was a workshop of sorts where creativity was encouraged and flourished via ample offerings of easels, palettes, brushes, paints, watercolors, crayons, paste, playdough, and clay.

Next door, the tiny bathroom was outfitted with child-sized toilets, shelves of books to help pass the time, a small step to reach the sink, and children's artwork gracing the walls!

The entrance to the kitchen was a restaurant-style swinging door with a round window that allowed adults to see the comings and goings of the kitchen. Toward the bottom of the door was a smaller hole so children could see too.

What was probably the former family room now served as a gathering area where we were offered couches, pillows, and beanbags. There was a flannel board, a piano, and rows and rows of books! So many books! *Mike Mulligan and His Steam Shovel, Where the Wild Things Are, The Little House, Caps for Sale, The Very Hungry Caterpillar, The Story of Babar: The Little Elephant* . . . books as far as I could see!

Across from this gathering area were the tables we used for activities and snack. Each was draped with a red-and-white checked tablecloth and surrounded by low benches. Mary used communal benches in lieu of individual chairs, a small, subtle way she encouraged language and social development. Behind the tables was the door that led to the covered back porch, and *there was more out there!*

The porch was a world all in itself. On one side there were boxes of dress-up clothes: capes, high-heeled shoes, feather boas, raincoats, a bunch of different kinds of shirts, fireman boots, construction hats, and party dresses. In the middle there were more art easels. A cotton string, the full length of the porch, was suspended above me. "The drying line," Mary said, "for your pictures." Long wooden brushes peeked out from orange juice cans serving as paint cups. More paint and extra brushes rested on the wooden cable spool that doubled as a table. At the other end of the porch was a waist-high wooden

Many years later, as an adult, I recalled a book from my time at Mary's Nursery School. All I could remember was that it was about a young boy who was eating a lot of pancakes and that it had many black-and-white photographs. With a nod to a gentleman who ran a bookstore in San Diego, I am pleased to report that he located the book, *Do You Know What I Am Going to Do Next Saturday?* by Helen Palmer. I reread it recently and am not sure if anyone would be willing to publish it nowadays, but let me tell you it's awesome!

sandbox filled with a kind of soft white sand that I can still smell if I close my eyes. Scoops, funnels, eggbeaters, flour sifters, wooden spoons, measuring cups, and muffin tins lay an arm's length away, waiting to be employed by a child's imagination.

Miss Mary opened the screen door that led from the porch to the backyard. Ahhh, the yard! Without any exaggeration I can say that, as a three-year-old, it was unlike any other I had ever seen! Here were swings, ladders, structures to climb, bikes to ride, hammers for pounding, ducks and chickens to chase, bunnies to hold, and water to splash. There were cable spools to roll and jump from, capes to wear, nails and wood for building things, baby dolls for washing, and a *boat*! A real boat for painting on and pretending in. There was a sandpit for digging with real shovels, bubbles for blowing, and right in the middle of the yard a tall metal slide that was hotter than Hades and as high as the sun.

We stood there together in the yard. I didn't move. I was taking it all in. Then she gently let go of my hand, bent down, and, in a voice I can still hear, once again looking me square in the eye, said, "Go play."

I burst onto the yard and spent the morning running around, climbing trees, playing tag, jumping through mud puddles, climbing a rope ladder, reading books, singing songs, splashing water, painting pictures . . . playing.

I would spend the next two years with my Miss Mary, Miss Nancy, and Miss Gerry. I would play hard, sing loud, and make mud pies. I would climb trees, run with friends, jump rope, and build blocks. I would listen to songs, make puppets, and draw pictures. Sometimes I would get mad and hit other kids, only to cry big tears when the same was done to me. I would make friends, push them away, and attempt to get my way by withholding invitations to a nonexistent party. I would be very loud and incredibly quiet. But today, this first day, while my shoes were still new and my lunch box still shiny, I would have snack.

No one could have possibly foreseen the impact this snack would have on my adult life. What do I mean? OK, so I was a pretty average kid, perhaps occasionally a little more talkative, sometimes more active, but overall a typical, playful little kid who enjoyed most of the traditional activities children enjoy. But I had an unusual favorite snack. Not grahams, not PB&Js, not applesauce or pretzels with oranges, but cheese. And not just regular cheese, but hot, spicy jalapeño pepper jack cheese. I could eat it on crackers, by itself, on bread, but my favorite way to enjoy it was with a slice of a crunchy red apple.

So here's what happened on my first day of school: At some point in the morning our play came to a halt with an *invitation* to come and have snack. I say *invitation* because no one was *required* to come in for snack, no threats were given if toys were not promptly put away, no general mandates to join the group at the table. Miss Mary sent an invitation through that dusty screen on the porch: "Come on in if you're hungry!"

I was hungry!

Her invitation prompted the hasty dropping of shovels and buckets back into the sandbox, the jumping of children off the tops of climbing equipment, hoses being shut off, easel brushes tossed back into paint cups, and bunnies returned to cages. It was time to eat. We had been playing all morning, and we were *starving*. We came inside, washed our hands, and sat down at the benches around the tables. We poured water or milk (our choice!) from small pitchers into small cups and passed around the napkins. As I took my napkin, the kitchen door swung open.

Miss Mary came out from the kitchen holding the big snack tray, and on it were piles of crunchy red apples and slices of hot pepper jack cheese. I just about fell out of my chair! Could this cheese be just for me? It was like being invited to a dinner party where the hostess made all your favorite foods because she wanted you to know how excited she was to have you there! I looked up at Miss Mary as she put the snack tray down in front of me. She leaned in toward me and whispered in my ear, "We are so glad you are here."

In that moment I had a very brief yet very powerful experience. I had a crystallizing moment: I knew then and there that I would become a teacher.

A CRYSTALLIZING MOMENT

Howard Gardner tells us that at any given moment of any given day we could be facilitating an experience that makes a lifelong impact. He calls this a "crystallizing moment." And as teachers, we never know when one might occur. Could be Monday, Friday, the rainy day, the day we are in a good mood, the day we are in a bad mood. We cannot plan, schedule, buy, or coordinate a crystallizing moment. There isn't a signal, a bell, or a loud trumpet indicating one has happened: "Crystallizing Moment! Room 5! GO! Go! Go!" Ideally, crystallizing moments occur when we are at our best. Unfortunately, for some, it's when an adult was at their worst. Crystallizing moments can be happy memories or sad ones. This is only one of the many reasons why we MUST be fully present when we are with children and must never never, ever ever underestimate the impact of what we do.

I highly doubt Miss Mary thought, "Boy, I bet this cheese is going to be a big hit with the new kid!" She was simply doing what she did best. She was aware of the children, our needs, our simple wishes, and our comfort. I'm sure the casual (probably routine) call she placed to my mom sounded something like this: "Hi Laura! We are getting ready for Lisa's arrival! Since Monday is her first day at school and her first day ever away from you, we want her to have a smooth transition, maybe provide something that she really likes for snack. What's her favorite?"

A two-minute phone call that made a lifelong impact. The *why* behind my work, the fire in my belly, and the passion in my heart can all be traced back to when Miss Mary came through that swinging kitchen door carrying the snack tray.

It all started with the cheese.

2

At Any Given Moment

MANY TEACHERS BECOME teachers because of a teacher they had. At some point in their educational experience they were blessed with someone who took some extra time, went that extra mile, offered support and encouragement, and did *something* that made a lifelong impact. Remember this! *Never ever ever underestimate the impact of what you do!* At any given moment of any given day *you* could make a lasting impression on someone. *You* could be facilitating a crystallizing moment! *You* could be their Miss Mary! *You* could be their pepper jack cheese!

I became a teacher because of Miss Mary. The time I spent with her is what inspired me to become what I am today. After I had started teaching, she told me once that she didn't do anything special. I told her in response that maybe she didn't, but she did what was *right*, and that is something special.

As I grew up, I knew I wanted to give back what I got. I knew that someday I would create a place where children could explore, create, and simply *be*—not be "getting ready" for something, not be "hurried up," not be forced or pressured to develop past their years—but to simply *be*.

I grew up, went to high school, college, and was sidetracked briefly by a short-lived acting career and a two-year stint at a performance college in Chicago. Yet while I was there, I found myself taking child development classes, watching children on weekends, taking nanny jobs, volunteering at the local Boys and Girls Club, and planning various activities for children in shelters and housing projects. These new interests started to take precedence over learning my lines for upcoming shows. It was only then that I mustered the courage to ask myself why I was not *doing* what I was obviously so passionate about.

It seemed I was ignoring my calling.

I needed to do something different.

I decided to leave Chicago and return to California. Once settled, I set my sights on being a preschool teacher. I sat still long enough to earn my degree and kept the vision of Miss Mary in my head. I daydreamed constantly about the school I would build—a place where grown-ups facilitated and guided in lieu of barking out orders and commands.

I would create a place where twenty-minute schedules would be replaced with long periods of uninterrupted free time and where timers and whistles would be tossed in the garbage. At *my* school, rule sheets would NOT be plastered all over the walls, and children would be able to play outside *all day* if they were so inclined.

I would be an advocate for children. I would try with all my might to never forget what it was like to be little. I would educate moms and dads and give them permission to trust their instincts and each other instead of being pressured to succumb to the wills of prying neighbors, meddling relatives, and the ever-present, powerful media when making choices for their children.

I would question what was served up as educational dogma and challenge "the way it had always been done." I would learn, grow, make mistakes, cry, scream, and laugh. I would read everything I could get my hands on and find people to talk with about it. I would ban product-oriented cut-out patterned art and would fire everyone who became a teacher because they like to tell little people what to do. But above all, I would give back to the children what Miss Mary gave me and would teach parents and other educators why play-based, hands-on learning is how children are getting ready for school!

I'm getting ahead of myself though.

This was going to take some time. My first real indication of the time it would take came when I began interviewing for my first teaching position. It became apparent that the early childhood educational environment in which I would start my career was very different from the one I experienced when I was a child.

Upon graduating from college, armed with my degree and my naïveté, I learned a few things right out of the gate: First, the *idealism* of lab schools and college campus children's centers stood in stark contrast to the *reality* of child care. Second, things such as bunnies and ducks in the yard, parents assisting at snacktime, covered porches, slides and swings, half-day programs, outside easels, and boats to paint were no longer the norm. Instead, early childhood environments were filled with long hours (for both teachers and children), no money for supplies, embalmed mail-order curriculum packets, patterned art bulletin boards, unspeakable wages, pressure to be ready for kindergarten, tired, overscheduled children, and frazzled parents. And third (the scariest of all my realizations), it seemed as though while I was in the business of growing up, going to school, and completing my degree, all the Miss Marys of the world had been mysteriously stolen away and replaced with the Laminated Ladies.

In 1991, I encountered my first Laminated Lady when I showed up at my very first teaching job and was introduced to the woman who was going to be my "mentor." She would, according to my director, "teach me what I needed to know."

She had lesson plans that were laminated . . . from 1975.

She was my first exposure to this very recognizable breed of teaching professionals. You find them on preschool playgrounds standing away from the children, spinning their whistle-on-a-rope, and waiting for the blessed time at which they can blow it to call the children in from recess. You can find them inside the classrooms too. They are the ones wearing keys around their necks, keys that open cupboards containing the playdough, paper, and markers. Many of them have twelve boxes lining the shelf on the back wall, each nicely labeled "January," "February," "March," and in each box are the activities to be done for each month, every month, with every class, every year. These teachers also tend to have (forgive my rudeness) a poopy-face.

Laminated Ladies have masking tape lines down the middle of the classroom to show children where to "line up" and name tags attached to the lunch table and a circle carpet to show children where to sit. Laminated Ladies have a schedule for snacktime, outside time, art time, lunchtime, and potty time. They are the bosses of naptime and the drill sergeants of circle time. In their world, preschool is boot camp for kindergarten.

I was astounded!

When I questioned what they were doing and why they taught like this, they told me, "Times have changed, Lisa! It's not all fun and games like it was when you were little. We have to *get the children ready for kindergarten* now! We must do *curriculum!*"

After three weeks at my new job, asking questions and getting nowhere except being put in a time-out (true story), my Laminated Mentor sat me down and informed me that I better just "get with the program!"

3

Getting with the Program

DURING MY EARLY months of teaching I started to realize I had so many questions. Not the least of which was, "What am I doing?!"

Where were the mud pits, shovels, story times, and upright pianos?

Am I going to make it?

Was play-based teaching *really* no longer accepted?

Had things *really* changed so much?

Did I *really* need to get with the program?

Why did I feel that I was the only one who thought things weren't right and should be different?

I felt very alone. I was dangling off the side of a cliff, frantically holding onto a teaching style I both received and remembered. I *refused* to forget what I got from Miss Mary, but I was not yet strong enough. I was unable to hold on by myself and had yet to meet the people who would have been able to help pull me up. So I fell. Down, down, down into the abyss with the Laminated Ladies, where, upon hitting bottom, I discovered smiles traded in for whistles, laughter exchanged for line-up lines, and hugs replaced with idle threats to "call your mother!"

I spent three years with the Laminated Ladies. I acquired my own whistle, my own roll of masking tape (and the line-up lines that went along with it), files of dittos and patterns, and, among other things, a basket of songs that included such favorites as "Wash, Wash, Wash Your Hands," "Traffic Lights," "Clean Up," and "Safety Belts," most of which were sung to the tune of either "Row, Row, Row Your Boat" or "Jingle Bells." I also gathered a collection of catchy phrases to use with children, such as these:

"I'm waiting!"

"Sit still!"

"SHHHH! Be quiet!"

"One, two, three! Eyes on me!"

"Get out of the bathroom!"

"Why are you wet?!"

And my personal (un)favorite, "Crisscross applesauce!"

I made huge construction paper STOP signs and posted them in activity centers to indicate to children a particular center was "closed." I strictly monitored seating arrangements via name tags that were contact-papered to tables, and spent many evening hours cutting out patterns for art and photocopying dittos for "table time."

It took three years of being in the abyss with the Laminated Ladies before I realized that "getting with the program" was not my cup of tea. Prior to this I may have had questions, but I didn't really search for answers. I simply got with the program. Now, I was ready to start digging for the answers that would inform the next phase of my professional growth. I started to question *everything*, including the educational practices that had been modeled to me. I started changing my mind about many aspects of teaching. I found new mentors. I read books about education, children, learning styles, and teaching philosophies. I surrounded myself with other folks who saw what I saw, questioned what I questioned, and were willing to embark on this journey with me. Some walked side by side with me, and some served as guides and mentors.

To paraphrase Obi-Wan Kenobi from the *Star Wars* movies, I had taken my first step into a larger world. I grew up a little and changed my mind a lot. I no longer cut out patterns or ran off dittos. I no longer said things like "Sit still and be quiet" because I knew that children did not need to sit on their bottoms with "eyes on me" in order to participate in the telling of a story. I ripped up my masking tape line-up line and threw it in the trash, but I kept the whistle to remind me of what I didn't want to be *ever again.*

As Vygotsky would have observed, those early years found me in my ZPD, my Zone of Proximal Development, due to the effective and caring—yet direct and noncompromising—scaffolding provided to me by the likes of Bev Bos, Michael Leeman, Tom Hunter, Dan Hodgins, Jenny Chapman, Cynde Scrimger Nichols, Sharron Krull, Barb Chernofsky, and Alfie Kohn, and many, many others. By exposing myself to new information and meeting people who were a bit farther down the path than myself, I was able to start changing my mind-set. And while these folks taught me more than I could ever properly acknowledge, I need to state that the lessons I learned from falling into the abyss were more powerful than if I had stepped around it. I do not regret my experience with the Laminated Ladies one bit, for they taught me what I *didn't want to be,* and for that I am forever grateful.

But let's be real. Change is hard. It takes time! I also know even just acknowledging that change is difficult can be easier said than done. But please know that I didn't just jump up and fly out of that abyss! Although I didn't have this phrase when I started out, I have it now, and I will share with you: The next time you find yourself faced with an opportunity to incorporate some new nugget of learning you've been exposed to, ask yourself, "What part of this can I say *yes* to?" This mind-set will help you as you take the baby steps that are required for real, effective, long-term change. What part of THIS—as small as it might be—might I be able to incorporate?

I tried new things, implemented new ideas, broke inappropriate habits, pushed myself out of my comfort zone, felt confident, assimilated the change, and took another step. I paused. I reflected. What is working? What is not? Real change takes time. It is *not* fast. Again, let me repeat, do not think it should be quick. Fast-paced superficial changes do not last, because they do not allow for a full understanding of why the change is necessary in the first place. There must be a process of increased awareness and personal discovery. As I like to say, we need to *reflect*, not *react*.

Such personal reflection allowed my initial journey to pick up momentum. I gained clarity and began to see the direction I wanted to go. It's been said that we go back to what we know first . . . it was time for me to go. My questions and search for answers took me *back* to Miss Mary and the teaching style I knew first.

4

Starting the Journey

NOT SURPRISINGLY, AS I began the journey of becoming the teacher I wanted to be, I realized there is always something new to learn, a new skill to obtain, a new article to ponder, and a more challenging book to read. But I didn't want to just gather up ideas, I wanted to *live them*! So I made a commitment to take the ideas I had collected from books—skills, activity ideas, and suggestions—and start putting them into practice. I wanted to make sure I was a part of a program that was giving children what they needed.

And what **do** they need? Well, among other things, they need adults who are paying attention. At the end of the day it all comes down to the relationships we cultivate with the children and their families. What else? Long periods of uninterrupted exploratory time, not twenty-minute time blocks that are regulated with kitchen timers. Clay and playdough, not pencils and computer keyboards. Mud, sand, and water, not dittos and work sheets. Lots of outside time, shovels, hammers, nails, and loose parts, not screens that blast the latest animated features and apps that promise to "make them smart."

If you asked them at the time, and perhaps still now, my administrators would say they were supportive of me, and in their defense, they were. However, the troubling thing about most preschools and child care centers is that policies and program decisions are typically *not* made by folks who have experience in child development. (I realize I am making a dangerous generalization here, yet will make it anyway.) Many administrators, owners, directors, and principals are either older-elementary people, meaning grade four and above, or are businesspeople. Please know they are often very good ones, but they are not child development people, and this is the root of much conflict.

Teachers want to provide engaging experiences and activities for the children. Owners want to keep the carpet clean. Teachers want to say, "Rip up the damn carpet!"

Many early childhood educators end up quitting due to frustration, while directors are frequently caught in the middle, playing referee between the demands and expectations of teachers, parents, and owners. As I began to question administrators, directors, site supervisors, and owners, I realized that lip service paid to "the needs of children" and "the power of play" and "developmentally appropriate practice" was not the same as *doing* it! They talked about it, wrote about it in the brochures, advertised it in the newspaper, and mentioned it during tours for prospective families, but very few were actually *doing* it.

All this disconnect and inconsistency aside, what became so incredibly frustrating and seemed to make matters worse was when "vigilante teachers" (as I started to be called) did it, our efforts were met with letters of reprimand, requests to "come into the office," and statements of "we don't do that here." The reality of the disconnect between theory and practice started to come across loud and clear.

The debates ensued: Teachers struggled with other teachers, directors with owners, teachers with owners, directors with teachers, and parents with teachers. At some point during the madness, I remembered a poster that was in my sociology professor's office that said, "When elephants fight, it is the grass that suffers." It was then I realized it was time for me to move on. I had, for lack of a better phrase, outgrown where I was. It was time to find a place where continued learning and questioning were permitted, where wonder and curiosity were more important than the carpet, and where I would have the freedom to deepen my exploration and understanding of developmentally appropriate practice, my teaching style, and my philosophy.

I have some hindsight is twenty-twenty commentary on this. If it should come to pass that you are ready to make a leap and the folks you are with are not yet ready, there is nothing wrong with that unless you continue to try to make them want it. Or see it. If you are well aware that you have hit the ceiling of your current program, you have a few options: one, pretend like you don't notice but go home every day in tears, get migraines, and eat ibuprofen all day; two, have a conversation with someone about where you find yourself in your professional journey and what you are feeling and observing; or three, quit.

My point is that you need to deal with your problem, as hard and as uncomfortable as it might be. Solving it might come later, but dealing with it, calling it out, kicking it around must happen. With all the love in my heart, I am telling you honestly and sincerely that you have no right to complain about ANYTHING if in fact you are not willing to do anything about it. In her amazing book *Swinging Pendulums: Cautionary Tales for Early Childhood Education*, author Carol Garhart Mooney reminds us that if we refuse to participate, then we relinquish our right to pontificate.

Breathe.

As I set my sights elsewhere, I had another quick realization. I realized there were not many programs out there where I "fit." Many child care centers were hiring, I could have gotten a job, but I wanted more. I wanted an environment where my philosophy and the school's philosophy matched! A place where as soon as you walk in, you say, "Yes! I belong here." Those places, however, are the places where the staff never leave, because they know they have got a good thing! So that was not an option. I didn't have the money to build a school or buy a school, so I did what seemed the next best thing and opened a family child care in my home.

5

A New Beginning

I MOVED INTO a house that had a huge yard with space for a garden, a sandbox, and a mud pit! The backyard was large enough for climbing equipment, but it also provided many nooks and crannies for independent play and exploration. The children ate the pomegranates that grew on the tree, the grapes that grew on the vine, and the wild raspberries that appeared one year along the back fence. We grew tomatoes and green beans, played in the dirt, and splashed in the water. The kids made adobe bricks by drying blocks of wet mud in the sun, and there were both independent and teacher-planned art choices offered daily.

We sang and danced, read books, painted pictures, built block towers, wrote stories, and watched the bugs scramble in and out of the garden. We froze water to make ice and then observed what happened when we put the ice in the sun. I succeeded in creating a place, as small as it might have been, where children were celebrated and their interests honored. It was energetic, child-centered, and play-based. I was pleased.

I began to document my observations of the children, their activity choices, the materials we used, and the things we "did" all day. I challenged myself to identify the *what* and the *why* in what I was observing in order to master the ability to articulate my belief system and philosophy. No longer excused from participating in debates and discussions because I was somehow "new" or "green," I came into my own as a professional educator and found it of utmost importance to be able to both support and sometimes defend what I was doing in the classroom. In hindsight I realize that while I was probably not aware of it at the time, I was internalizing the power and importance of being able to articulate the intentions behind my educational choices. I started collecting articles, journals, and books that guided my classroom decisions. It was way back then that I began my personal and professional journey of linking what I was doing with data and research that supported it. As I look back, the Binder Challenge I mentioned in the opening of this book started a long time ago when I first proposed it to myself.

The documentation process I adopted led me to rethink lesson planning. It now made sense to plan activities based on what I was observing, rather than simply providing random activities pulled from resource books. Until this realization, I prepared lesson plans in accordance with the unwritten code of traditional lesson planning. Here is the planning recipe I was given and expected to follow (and did) until I had my aha moment:

Lesson Planning

INGREDIENTS:
- one weekend a month
- pen
- mounds of "activity books"

WHAT TO DO:
Give up one weekend a month. Plow through resource books for two days until you find enough activities for the upcoming month. Fill in the blanks of a lesson plan book. Pick out a few highlights to post on the calendar that will be prominently displayed on the classroom wall. Photocopy this calendar for the parents (ideally to be posted on refrigerators as reminders of field trips and other schoolwide activities but rarely making it beyond the backseat or floor of the car). Try to overlook the latter. Submit the lesson plan book to the director for review. Do the activities you said you would do. Repeat next month. And the next. And the next.

Whether spoken or implied, this is what is expected. Unless of course you work in one of those places where the curriculum and lessons come in the mail from a corporate office fifteen hundred miles from your center. In this case you simply do, month after month, what the man who sits behind the desk tells you to do. But I'm getting ahead of myself. . . .

As I embarked down the journey of rethinking lesson planning and themes, I read a lot about emergent curriculum, theme webbing, child-initiated themes, and the project approach. I watched how different classrooms handled themes and lesson planning and spoke with teachers who said their schools had stopped using them. I inquired, questioned, and outlined a new system. I did not simply wake up one morning and, in a fit of Sunday laziness, decide not to do lesson plans anymore! I did the work and research first and then defined my new process: I use my observations of what *the children* are interested in to determine my next course of action. The children became the boss of the process, not me. I started to see what *facilitate* versus *instigate* really meant.

What exactly does this mean? It means that instead of getting your activity ideas from a book, you get them from the children. It means teachers watch what children are doing and use the information gathered from their observations to extend or deepen what is unfolding in front of them. I began walking around with a little notebook in my pocket and a pen around my neck, making notes, documenting observations, patterns, issues—what were they telling and showing me that they needed from this place, and how could I get that for them?

A classroom that abandons the traditional agonizing monthly lesson-planning ritual in exchange for the preparation of meaningful activities based on documented observations shows a commitment to both the development of the children and the quality of the program. A classroom that merely stops lesson planning because it's dumb, time consuming, or boring shows a lack of commitment and dedication not only to the profession but also to the children.

The *children* are the curriculum. Objective and detailed observation of the children's desires, activity choices, interests, passions, and challenges will provide educators with all the curriculum they will ever need. Curriculum does not come out of activity and resource books. These books are just that, *resources*. They are tools to be used in conjunction with your observations in order to deepen the explorations happening in the program. They are *not* the program.

Authentic, meaningful curriculum does not come in a kit you buy at a conference or a prepackaged box that arrives in the mail. How could someone working in an office that is a thousand miles from your home or school have any inkling as to what your children need in their environment right now? How is a mail-order unit on snow applicable to a family child care home in San Diego? How are mandated lesson plans from a corporate office in Kansas City really meaningful to a group of inner-city preschoolers in Seattle? They aren't. They are not meaningful; they are just easy. These prepackaged kits make life easier and present a facade of program planning when all they really do is serve as a substitute for active involvement with the children.

Additionally, they are insulting. These kits have gone from suggested lessons and activities to scripts. Scripts for teachers working with any grade or age group are an insult to our ability, profession, intelligence, and talent. Anyone can sit in a chair and read a script. If we have reached a point where curriculum needs to be "teacher proof," and teachers are not trusted to be able to practice the art and craft of true teaching, let's face it, we have a much bigger problem.

I am proud to say that in the end I opted for meaningful instead of easy. I stopped the monthly agonizing ritual of filling in the blanks of lesson plan books with random activities, circle time games, and science projects. Instead, I sat with my teaching journal after the children went home and reflected on what we had done that day.

I made time every day for open-ended, process-oriented art projects. There were easels inside and out. We sang songs together. I read stories to them, and they read to each other. Some children began writing their own stories. Instead of ignoring behavior problems or ineffectively dealing with them via "time-outs," we talked through them, discussed our feelings, and planted the seeds for effective communication skills. We rolled up our sleeves to squish and explore lots of sensory experiences. We had time outside for lots of running around, gardening, watching birds fly overhead, catching roly-poly bugs, playing parachute games, climbing trees, jumping off big boulders, and eating grapes and berries right off the vines. And all of this was executed with a playful spirit.

I started asking myself, "What did we do today?" And I wrote it all down. After some time, being one who locks and loads on patterns, my documentation revolved around seven words: create, move, sing, discuss, observe, read, and play. At the end of each day I asked myself, "Did we make time today to do these things?" If we did, then I wrote down how. If not, I documented possible reasons as to why not. I slowly began to see that *play* (as a category) was not a separate seventh thing, because all of the things we were doing could be classified as play or playful.

THe seven THinGS

The Seven Things (as they came to be called) became the framework through which we planned our program. Everything I did with the children was grounded in one of the Seven Things, and everything overlapped. It is important to note that I wasn't doing anything different than before, I just started to see that the experiences and activities could be categorized and classified.

> NOTE: The list of Seven Things was not and is not a checklist! It was not like the children came in each morning and I said, "Here's a brush, paint a picture!" (create, check!), "OK, now let's sing a song!" (sing, check!), "Come over here and look at the bird nest Peter brought in!" (observe, check!). Get my meaning? **This is very important!** Each of the Seven Things is not something to "do" for the sake of doing only to then hurry on to "do" the next one.

I used my observations to plan for the next day. For many, initially, this seems backward. Allow me to say that we still had things out and available. And within reason and with a healthy dose of risk assessment and common sense, the children decided the where, when, and how of what they did. I then linked my observations to the Seven Things. Dress-up, blocks, writing, sensory tubs, science, art, manipulatives, books, and outdoor play were always available. I started to refer to these centers as "the bones," and the bones were always available. My job was to add to, extend, and otherwise deepen and facilitate a child's interaction with other children and with the materials within the room (and the bones) throughout the course of the day. I used my observations from the day to plan for the next day.

This sometimes meant going to a curriculum or resource book to gather an idea or two to deepen or extend something the children had shown interest in, *not because I needed an activity to fill a time slot*. Sometimes it would mean adding extra materials. I know this now to be called a *provocation*. A provocation is something intentionally added to the space to invite children to investigate further. Sometimes it was simply adding something to an area that was already established. For example, maybe I would put magnifying glasses or goggles beside the trays of seashells that we collected on our trip to the beach. Or perhaps I would make different kinds of paper available during art time because fingerpainting was the favorite art experience right now, and I might have been wondering (aloud or silently), how might the project be different if we fingerpainted on foil instead of paper? Or wax paper? Shiny paper? Construction paper? If my notes indicated that two children who rarely used the sandbox were suddenly interested in it, instead of trying to figure out *why* they were suddenly so interested, I would simply put extra buckets and shovels near the sandbox to facilitate their new interest and encourage their continued exploration.

I was the facilitator. My job was to provide the children with the time and materials they needed to deepen and further their explorations within the environment. I made sure the bones were provided, gave the children ample time to explore, and kept linking my observations to the Seven Things. Documentation of how the children spent time each day PLAYFULLY creating, moving, singing, discussing, observing, and reading became the foundation upon which we built the program.

6

Teach Us to Read!

AFTER MY FAMILY child care program had been up and running for a while, the group of children who had been with me from the start (those who had followed me from the Laminated Lady Preschool Center to my home program) began to turn four, four and a half, and five years old. One day, out of the blue, they began asking me to teach them how to read.

It really took me by surprise! I told them they didn't need to know how to do that . . . yet. "Go play!" I said. But they insisted I show them. I insisted they go and play! We went round and round. So, needing guidance myself, I turned to my bookshelf and reread what Vivian Paley, Bev Bos, Maria Montessori, and Sydney Gurewitz Clemens had to say about this.

Would "teaching reading and writing" be an acceptable activity in a self-professed play-based, child-centered environment? Could I—and more importantly, *would* I—still be those things if we went down this path, or would it hurl me into the realm of those "academic hurry-up-and-get-them-ready" programs that I so loathed? I had so many questions! I spoke with colleagues, read articles, and even flipped through the pop-culture parenting magazines while deciding what to do. I found myself questioning why I viewed their request to read and write so differently than their prior requests for, say, cornstarch, more paper, fresh paint, or a new story. Why was this so different?

I was, once again, at another crucial point in my professional journey. After many weeks of thinking, reading, talking, and investigating, I adopted the "reading program" that Sydney Gurewitz Clemens references in her book *The Sun's Not Broken, a Cloud's Just in the Way*. And while I imagine her essay on the trials and tribulations of working with inner-city children in a San Francisco preschool was not intended to be a guide for teaching reading, the method she described spoke to me. It seemed right. So I adopted it. Years later I read Sylvia Ashton-Warner's *Teacher* and learned about the "organic reading" system she developed in her native New Zealand. The two methods are quite similar, and I think it is important to acknowledge them both.

I was not a literacy expert, so I trusted my gut and went with my first instinct—the children were asking me to teach them to read, so I asked them what they *wanted* to read. In my naïveté (again), it seemed to me that if the children were expressing a desire to read and write, they might have something specific in mind they wanted to read or write about!

So with apologies to Sydney and Sylvia for reducing their work to a paragraph, here is what we did. One at a time, I invited the children who had self-proclaimed a desire to read to tell me the word(s) they wanted to know. Then I wrote these words down on three-by-five-inch cards. The children kept their individual word cards in their very own word envelopes, which were neatly stacked on the table *they* designated as "the reading table." During the day some of the children would opt to spend time at the "reading table," just as they would spend time looking at picture books, building with blocks, painting pictures, and squeezing playdough.

It became immediately obvious that the words they wanted to know were words that had context to their daily experiences! Right in line with what educator Jane M. Healy states in her book *Endangered Minds*: children attach words to their experiences. I was watching her words unfold in front of my eyes.

The children who had been with me the longest were the ones who were excited about continuing to add words to their word envelopes. To these children I taught (with apologies to literacy specialists) what I called the "connector words." Words such as *at, the, to, or, and* . . . the "little words," if you will, that allowed them to create sentences. The kids would line up the words, make real sentences and nonsense ones, and would read their sentences to the kids sitting with them at the table. The more words they added to their envelopes the more obvious the link between experiences and words became.

All of the children who had word envelopes wanted to read *daddy, mommy, house,* and *dog*. This wasn't very surprising, as they each had one! The only child who wanted to read *baby* was the child with the new baby sister. One child had an older brother who was very involved with motocross bike racing; his weekends were spent with his family watching his older brother race dirt bikes. Interestingly, his word envelope contained words such as *blood, jump, hill, helmet, BBQ, trailer, desert, hot,* and *crash*. He was three. Was he reading? Yes. Anything wrong with that? No. Except that BLOOD does not appear on any kindergarten sight-word list or word wall I've ever seen. Which is too bad. If we allowed children to read from material that had context to their experience, their choices might be considered "nontraditional," but I would venture to guess that everyone would be just as amazed as I was in regard to their interest, progress, and ability.

So we read. The process continued. The connection between language, words, and experiences became very apparent. Younger children would declare their intention to read, so we would start a word envelope for them, but their interest didn't last. They weren't ready—*the direct experiences need to come first*. Later on they would attach the words. Those with word envelopes were never ever forced to participate in this "reading process," and we didn't make a big deal out of those who did. We did not advertise our program as one that would "teach your child to read!" We did not list "reading skills" or "writing strategies" on our informational brochure. A child who had started a word envelope was not coerced or directed to "spend some time with his cards." It was just another part of what we did at the program, no different from the mud pit, the dress-up area, the sandbox, the stacking pegs, or the block zone. After years of providing experiences, many of the children were ready to start attaching words to them.

The first group moved on to kindergarten, and within a few months the calls began. I was not expecting these calls. My family child care colleagues were not getting these calls. These were calls from kindergarten teachers asking me what I had been *doing* with the children all day. Teachers announced to me that some of the children who had been in my program were walking around their new classrooms saying things like, "Been there, done that! Been there, done that!" One teacher specifically demanded to know what I had been "doing with them." A typical call went something like this:

"What were they doing all day with you?"

"Playing," I said.

"No, really."

"Really! We spent most of the day playing."

"What do you mean, *playing*?"

"We read stories and books, we sang lots of songs, painted pictures, played in the mud, ran around, played tag, planted a garden, did lots of science, squished shaving cream, played in the water each day, went on some field trips, you know, the usual preschool stuff."

"But some of them are *reading*."

"Some of them were ready."

"Yes, but what did you *do*?"

"We played."

Clearly we were getting nowhere.

What was my secret? What did I do? Was there a special diet? No dairy? Lots of fish? Oh please, do tell the source of the expensive curriculum package you must have surely ordered from an educational guru! "Tell us!" they demanded!

I hung up.

Of course they were doing well in school! Why did people seem so surprised? These children had been given the time to be children and to do the things that children do. They played! And by having spent years doing so, they went on to elementary school ready for more because their foundation was so strong!

And it was then that I had my most major aha moment, my epiphany, my "Eureka!" The foundation of play supports later learning!

I know we all *know* this, but I was now a firsthand witness. No longer was I simply regurgitating research-based facts to appease the naysayers. My own awareness was becoming clearer. We all know that a building needs a foundation or it will fall down. *Playing* is the foundation that supports a child's house of learning. The foundation is made up of all the things we had been making time for the children to do: creating, moving, singing, discussing, observing, and reading. Playing was the cement that held it all together.

All of a sudden I saw so clearly what I had been reading about. I had made some long strides on my journey, but this was a huge leap for me. All of a sudden what I was really put here to do became very clear. I felt a call to develop this idea further. I continued to make time each day to do the Seven Things and also started an in-depth exploration of *why*. How could I start linking the Seven Things to the research?

I knew this exploration would encourage me to continue growing personally and professionally. It would increase my knowledge, strengthen my program, and allow me to support my views while speaking with teachers, parents, providers, and school administrators. I was walking the walk and learning how to talk the talk. I was gathering fuel for my fire; I was reading everything I could get my hands on, attending workshops and seminars and discussing views with colleagues. So in 1996 I decided to attend the National Association for the Education of Young Children's (NAEYC) annual conference. For any educator, this is a huge time and financial commitment. That year it took place in Dallas. I registered, rented a car, booked the hotel, and jumped on a plane with no clue as to how it would change my life.

7

Strengthening the Foundation

SO IN 1996 I attended the NAEYC annual conference in Dallas. On the morning of the first day, a workshop was being offered that promised over a hundred hands-on activities for your sensory table, and handouts with recipes would be provided.

Stop the presses, people! Seriously, you don't even know. Back in the day HANDOUTS and especially ones with RECIPES would cause a stampede at any early childhood conference! Everyone attending the conference that morning was going to attempt to squeeze into this workshop! For what it's worth, any workshop having to do with art, science, hands-on activities, or sensory play turns teachers into crazy people. This conference was no exception.

An hour before start time the room was already filled with anxious attendees. There was a line out the door of people trying to get in. It looked like opening night of a highly anticipated movie release (or a new iPhone!). I was in the back of the line that extended into the hallway but KNEW I needed to get in. Pretending I knew someone inside, I proceeded to squeeze and 'scuse me my way into the room. After working my way down the aisle of chairs and through the sea of people, I approached the front row—BINGO! An empty chair right in the front! I sat down and introduced myself to the people around me. The room was buzzing with excitement. You could feel the energy! Everyone was anxiously awaiting the handout, which was sure to be filled with tons of new ideas. So we waited. And we waited. And waited.

Suddenly someone shouted, "Hey! Where's the presenter?"

Just then, a NAEYC representative approached the podium. "Umm," she said, tapping the microphone, "hi, I'm one of the conference volunteers, and I'm sorry to say that we don't know where the presenter is. We knew that this was going to be a popular workshop, and, well, since there are so many of you here, let's give her a few more minutes."

She left the riser. People started whispering; they were getting restless. Where was she? Where was her stuff? Where were the activity demos? Where was the hands-on stuff? Where were our HANDOUTS? I tapped the arm of the woman sitting to my left. "Geez," I half-jokingly said, "I could talk about this kind of stuff. I do it every day with the kids at school!" She looked at me "Well, why don't you get up there then?" I looked back. I was silent. I paused, and then said, "All right, I will!"

So I did. I got up on the riser, took the microphone, and said, "HELLO, my name is Lisa Murphy, and I am NOT the presenter." (I didn't have the handouts.) "I was expecting a workshop filled with new ideas for messy, squishy stuff for my sensory tub—is that what most of you were expecting?"

Seven hundred heads nodded up and down indicating, "YES!"

"Well," I continued, "I am a family child care provider in California. I do a lot of hands-on stuff every day with my kids. So, since the presenter isn't here, I thought I could share with you some of the things I do. Sound OK?" (Again, they nodded.)

There was a minute of chaos, and then we started. To be honest, the next hour is really a blur. I don't really remember what I said or what I told them. But based on the dozens of letters I received for months after the conference, I think it's safe to say that it was informative and applicable! I know I shared some of my favorite messy things to do. I'm sure I told a few stories, shared some things that worked and some things that didn't. I solicited ideas from the crowd, and everyone who wanted to say something did.

Workshop participants were asking questions, laughing, and frantically writing down all the ideas that were being shared. The energy was great. The time flew by, and as we wrapped things up, I thanked them all. Thanked them for sticking with me, for sharing their stories, suggestions, and activity ideas, and most of all, thanked them for allowing me such an amazing opportunity. Then with no prompting or signal or anything, they all stood up. They clapped, they cheered, they offered me jobs, and even asked if they could come see my school! They stayed after and asked me questions, and a few people yelled out, "Do you have a book?" I was awestruck, amazed, and about six feet off the ground.

Throughout the rest of the conference as I walked through the halls attending sessions, I heard, "There she is, there she is! That's the young woman who just got up and *did* it when the presenter didn't show up!" I was beaming. The lesson here, though, and what I took with me from Dallas, was the true understanding of what is meant by "the more you give, the more you receive." It would have been easy to have jumped up on the stage, "done" the workshop, enjoyed the ego stroke, and then gone home. I knew I had to do more, though. I felt (and still do feel) as though an opportunity was placed in front of me and I decided to grab it and run!

So the *end* of the conference was the *beginning* of my new adventure. I flew home from Dallas knowing that it was time to do something. It was time to start giving back; it was time for something more. And while perhaps a bit presumptuous, I honestly thought that if folks got excited about something I *made up*, what might happen if I did my homework? So that's what I did. I joined professional associations, asked questions, attended workshops, and started subbing for various programs in town. Here's why: I figured if someone was going to give me their attention and time, what I gave them in return needed to be timely and relevant and WORTH their time.

About six months after the life- and career-changing experience in Dallas, I started my company. I called it the Learning Through Adventure Company (to this day this is why my e-mail is LTAC@ooeygooey.com). Why did I call it this? Because I had a paper from when I was a young adult that had a floor plan for a nursery school drawn out, and on it I had written, "We are learning through adventure at lisa's nursery school."

So it was under this name that I started doing workshops at weekend early childhood conferences.

A short while later it became necessary to close the family child care program and relocate to a small cottage in San Diego, where I continued working with children by subbing and mentoring in local preschools but spent most of my time focused on developing my workshops. The occasional weekend presentation at local child development conferences had morphed into an exciting full-time professional business. I was invited by many wonderful schools, agencies, and individuals to conduct in-service trainings, community seminars, and conference keynotes all over the country. These speaking engagements allowed me to bring my message of child-centered teaching and the importance of the foundation of play to thousands of teachers, parents, family child care providers, and school administrators. While doing so, I connected with my personal commitment to assist educators in rekindling the fires in their own bellies and the passion in their own hearts. I wanted to help them remember why they get up every morning and do what they do.

While the cottage was nice, it was very small and my business was growing fast. There were computer monitors on the kitchen table, file cabinets in the dining room, client information taped to the mirror in the living room, and product assembly tables lined up in the bedroom. I wanted to do family child care again, and the speaking business obviously needed room to grow, so I found a larger house and began enrolling babies, toddlers, and preschoolers. I hired some great staff to assist me, as I was doing family child care during the day and seminars and workshops in the evenings and each weekend.

I worked diligently to make sure that the program became a working representation of what I was out on the road talking about. I wanted to see the philosophy in action. Initial ideas about the importance of play and the Seven Things were previously not much more than brainstorms scribbled in notebooks and on walls to eventually "do something with." Now they were transitioning into a philosophical framework. The making of time each day to create, move, sing, discuss, observe, read, and play no longer served simply as a guideline for classroom observation and planning. Within the Seven Things, I found the ingredients of a strong early childhood program, future school success, and a love of lifelong learning. Years of observations, along with a thorough investigation of the research, uncovered the vital importance that early experiences have on the lives of children.

It was time to start spreading the word.

When Does the Playing Stop?

EVEN THE MOST basic academic database search, and shoot, let's be honest, even a Google search, on the keyword *play* will provide the evidence our *heads* so desperately need in order to support what our *hearts* have known for years, that playing is the foundation of children's learning.

When children attend high-quality programs that are committed to nurturing relationships, use research to guide their practice, and plan activities and experiences that target all four developmental domains within early childhood, we say they are developmentally appropriate. In "early childhood speak" we call this engaging in "developmentally appropriate practice" (DAP). The four domains within DAP are cognitive development, language/literacy development, physical (large- and small-motor) development, and social/emotional development. Unfortunately, many providers and programs have felt pressure to focus on only one or two of the domains, most specifically, cognitive and language/literacy development. Many programs have become lopsided, sacrificing physical and social/emotional development in the name of readiness. So while it would be inaccurate to say that one domain is more important than another, it is accurate to say that in many programs social/emotional development and physical development need some extra attention to bring program planning back into balance after having had a developmentally inappropriate skill and drill, academic, hurry-up-and-get-them-ready orientation.

Somewhere along the way we forgot that early childhood environments that are grounded in DAP and that embrace playful learning *are* getting children ready for school.

Some of us worry that children will get "stuck" in the playing part and will never move on, never amount to anything, and, God forbid, might still be "just playing" when they are forty! This reminds me of a woman I encountered at a workshop I was doing. She stood up in the back row and frantically shouted, "But *when*, just *when* does the playing *stop*?"

I calmly told her, "Hopefully never."

People worry that when we allow children to play, we are depriving them of something—something more important. That somehow their education is being compromised and no longer "of quality." I worry that having reduced what we call "education" to the accumulation of random facts and test scores, it is no longer a "quality" anything. In his book *Brain Rules*, author John Medina tells us that if you want to make sure the child experiences the complete *opposite* of what is needed in order to learn, put them in school.

I have been told by some that in *their day* children were expected to go to school and learn to read, write, and do arithmetic. No attention was given to *playing* in the classroom, "We did what needed to be done!" True. I do not doubt this. It is, however, very important to point out that in *their day*, they also had, roughly, a good six or seven years of playing *prior to entering the classroom*! Playing in the neighborhood was how children "got ready for school." And I think it would be fair to say that if we teased apart their various experiences in the neighborhood, we could link much of what they did to the four domains of DAP.

It would be silly to turn a blind eye to the fact that while children have not changed, many social conditions have. Many children do not have the "growing up playing in the neighborhood" experience that their parents and grandparents did. Because of this, the free play, polliwogs and tadpoles, bike riding, stick ball, kick the can, jump rope, sandboxes, picnics, family outings, fishing, mud pies, lemonade stands, climbing trees, vacant lots, tree forts, loose parts, dress-up, and construction play need to be replicated in the early childhood environments where today's children *are* growing up.

Of course our parents and grandparents were reciting, memorizing, and doing sums in first and second grade! They had *six years* of play that created a strong foundation upon which were built the walls and windows of reading, writing, and arithmetic! The foundation of playful learning must come first.

Children today are not being given the same opportunity to develop at their own natural pace. They are expected to start "learning" and "performing" as soon as they emerge from the comfort and protection of the womb. The competition begins immediately, and it is *fierce*. "How much did he weigh?" "Is she rolling over yet?" "Does he sleep through the night yet?" "Can she tie her shoes?" "Which preschools was he accepted into?" Children are stripped of their right to play because of inappropriate pressure to begin accumulating a bunch of tricks they can then show off as though they were a part of a dog and pony show! "Count to fifty for Mrs. Barnes," "Tell Mr. Davis your colors," "Show Grandpa what a good speller you are!" "Play your new song on the piano for Auntie Beth!" "Dance for Grandma!" "Show Daddy your flash cards," "Sit!" "Jump through the hoop!" "Roll over!" "Play dead!" "Speak—woof woof!"

Congratulations, your education has begun. Here is your biscuit. Good dog.

> **THis is a GReat exeRcise.**
>
> Without thinking too hard or too long about it, take two minutes and jot down on a piece of paper a list of the things you remember doing as a kid. Next, go through the items on your list one by one, and consider where they fit within DAP. You'll notice that it is almost impossible for something to fit within only one single domain of development. You're probably also realizing that everything children historically engage in is grounded in developmentally appropriate practice. Historically, daily play experiences have contributed to children's learning.

When there is pressure to build a house without regard to the foundation that supports it, *it will fall down*. The same is true with our house of higher learning! Play is not just an idle waste of time. We must stop thinking of playtime as time being taken away from something else, something deemed (by grown-ups) as "more important." Phrases such as "academic preparation" and "school readiness" should be banned from conversations unless all parties agree to the definition of said phrases. Play supports school readiness and is not separate from learning. A foundation of creating, moving, singing, discussing, observing, and reading is held together by play. Play, once again, is the cement holding the foundation together, and it is this foundation that will, in turn, support the house of higher learning.

We all want what is best for children. But what we are often *sold* as best has nothing to do with what children really need. Kits and packages designed to make your child Better! Faster! Stronger! Smarter! are nothing more than products that people get paid to sell. Contrary to what marketing and advertising departments claim in glossy magazine spreads and during high-pressure radio spots, *they do not care about your children*. They prey on your *emotions*, your *concerns*, and your *desire* to do what is best for your children in order to *sell you their product*. All they really care about is your credit card number. We *all* want to see our children in big, grand, academic houses. But when we begin building walls, windows, and second stories on a weak or absent foundation, what is going to happen? Having all the good intentions in the world cannot make up for the fact that there is little or no support holding up our structure.

Play is the foundation of children's learning.

9

Meaningful Experiences

ADDING AND SUBTRACTING come *after*

* ☆ counting of roly-poly bugs in the grass,
* ☆ listening to sound patterns made by pots, pans, and rhythm sticks, and
* ☆ figuring out if there are enough oranges for everyone at the snack table.

Adding and subtracting does *not* come from memorizing sums from flash cards.

Writing comes *after*

* ☆ squishing of playdough,
* ☆ squirting spray bottles to make prints on the fence,
* ☆ using three million sheets of paper for scribbling shapes and spirals, and
* ☆ banging of marker tips, over and over again, on hundreds of sheets of paper.

Writing does *not* come by purchasing lined paper and chubby pencils.

Reading comes *after*

- ✩ hearing many stories while sitting on a comfortable lap,
- ✩ learning how to hold a book right side up, and
- ✩ having experiences that were often mirrored in favorite books.

Not by purchasing "how to teach your baby to read" DVDs.

As educators, we must find the balance between the extremes of "Activity Annies," who don't do much more than provide children with "cute" activity ideas gathered up at last weekend's conference, and "Laminated Ladies," with their whistles, timers, letter-of-the-day dittos, and colors-of-the-week work sheets. Often, when we start to change our minds about our practice, our pendulums swing too far in the opposite direction. So again, I implore you—take your time. Reflect. Resist the urge to react. Be patient. It can take years for a pendulum to find a center ground where the theory and practice are finally one and the same.

Challenge yourself to continue growing and learning while also finding your center point. And above all, stay committed to deepening your understanding of the playful learning philosophical orientation you claim to embrace.

Your willingness to allow children time to create, move, sing, discuss, observe, read, and play doesn't matter a hill of beans if you do not increase your willingness to link these activities to DAP. What does this mean? Well, it means a couple of things. First, it increases your ability to see that when children are engaged in playful experiences, they are still learning important concepts. Second, it increases your ability to link *concepts* to the *experiences* children are having. The *linking* of concepts to experiences assists children in understanding their world and how it works. (It also helps the naysayers to see that environments that encourage playful learning *are* getting children ready for school!)

When the children jump off rocks, we mention "gravity." When they see flubber oozing out of a suspended berry basket and slowly drip toward the floor, we mention it again. When balls go up and then come down, we say it yet again. I do not expect preschoolers to "get it," but I do know that if experiences that are relevant to them are linked regularly to language and vocabulary, the memory of the experience will trigger understanding when the concept is brought up again as they move on to elementary school. Out of these experiences come words, language, and an understanding of the concepts. But the *experience* is the starting spot. And the experiences need to be *real*.

What is my vested interest in learning how to sort rocks by color or size, line them up, count them, or spell R-O-C-K if I have never held a small one, never climbed on a huge one, never gathered any at the beach, never felt with my fingers how some are so very rough and some are smooth like glass, never gone on a hike and collected a few, or never thrown one into a puddle and counted the ripples? Children learn in the here and now!

In their book *Developmental Continuity across the Preschool and Primary Grades*, authors Nita Barbour, Carol Seefeldt, and Patricia Scully inform us that children do not have the capability to think abstractly until they are almost twelve years old. Therefore, every time we expect children to be interested in things (concepts, themes, activities, or ideas) they cannot see, touch, taste, hear, or smell right here and right now, we are expecting something that is developmentally *inappropriate*.

Let me put it plainly. Too many people are making inappropriate demands of young children, and then, when the children don't "get it," the adults push harder. You don't need to attend a professional development seminar on how to get toddlers to sit for circle time. You need to be thinking about why a two-year-old is being expected to sit still in the first place.

I constantly ask, "Can I bring *it* to them, or them to *it*?" If the answer is no, *it* does *not* belong in an early childhood classroom, and, as a gentle reminder, early childhood is defined as *birth* to age eight!

So, if it does not snow in the winter where you live, why would you spend time talking with children about it?

You might say, "But Lisa, we talk about snow EVERY December!" And I am going to lovingly say, "Why? You don't HAVE any!"

If you *insist* on talking about SNOW to children who live in San Diego because it is winter (as an example), you have two options, either find someone to truck some snow down from a mountain, or take a trip to the snowy mountain with the children and their families. If, however, neither of these is a plausible option, you need to ask, *Why you are talking about snow in the first place?* A sensory tub filled with grated ivory soap is not snow! It's soap! White playdough is not snow! It's playdough! Ice is not snow! It's ice. To children who have never touched, seen, smelled, or tasted snow, these activities are nothing more than abstract associations forced upon them by adults!

Here's an example. Years ago, a teacher who attended one of my seminars in Phoenix approached me on the break saying, "I gotta tell you something! It's about the idea of it needing to be real. I was raised back East but my children were raised here in Phoenix, and every December their teachers would make playdough snowmen and big white coffee-filter snowflakes to hang on the walls and decorate the classroom. I finally said forget it! Next December, we are going to Philly so they can see the real thing! So we get to Philly in December, and one morning it's snowing hard! I woke the kids up, and we go on the porch to watch, and as my five-year-old daughter comes outside, she looks up at the sky, and her face simply fell. She looked disgusted! I didn't know why! I told her, 'Look, honey, look! Look at the snowflakes!' And my daughter instead looked at me and said, 'Mama, the ones in Phoenix are so much bigger.'"

I rest my case.

The daughter, who for five years was exposed to six-inch, twelve-inch, and even jumbo-sized twenty-four-inch coffee-filter snowflakes, thought for sure she was being cheated when she saw the real "little ones" in Philly.

The *real* must come first! All subsequent abstract understanding is based on an initial experience of that which was initially touched, smelled, tasted, seen, or heard. If you want it in their head, it must start in their hand. And if you want it in their hand, it must begin from the heart. This mean their *interests* are where planning and curriculum begins—not from an activity book.

Adults need to strengthen their ability to link conceptual language to the playful experiences they provide to children on a daily basis. What does this mean? It means we don't stop fingerpainting in the name of readiness. Instead, we get better at articulating what is happening when a child *is* fingerpainting. Environments that advocate for playful learning are constantly connecting concepts to experiences.

Apples provide a great example. Let's say next week you are talking about apples (for a reason I HOPE you can identify, but that, as we say, is a different workshop). Answer these questions:

* ✶ What conceptual words can you attach to the experience as children cut the apple? *(dividing, math, estimating, small-motor development, confidence, risk taking, life skills)*

* ✶ As they make applesauce? *(more math, counting, kitchen chemistry, measuring, changing from a hard solid apple into mushy sauce, trying new foods)*

* ✶ As they count the seeds? *(math skills and small-motor development to grasp them and pick them up)*

* ✶ When they plant the seeds? *(gardening, patience, importance of water and sun, caring for a living thing)*

* ✶ As they are cutting apples in half to make apple prints on paper with paint? *(creativity, science, color mixing, fine-motor development, art)*

* ✶ When they are cutting the apples in half the other way to see the star? *(observation, differences, similarities)*

* ✶ When they are charting and graphing on paper who likes green ones, yellow ones, or red ones? *(math, estimating, counting)*

Think of the *language* you would hear in a classroom filled with preschoolers whose teacher brought in basket after basket of real apples for them to experience. Imagine, if you will, that the teacher wrote on the board all the words she heard the children calling out and saying to themselves and to each other as they ate their apples:

red!	bruised!	crunchy!
sour!	sweet!	sticker!
green!	stem!	worm!
hole!	seeds!	star!
juicy!	dry!	mushy!
smooth!	bumpy!	sticky!
tart!	hard!	nasty!
smell!	big bite!	taste!
smooth!	small!	big!
color!	shiny!	yellow!
round!	leaf!	skin!

Now imagine if the exploration of the same apple was limited to coloring books, dittos, identical paper-plate apples displayed on the bulletin board, a few apple books on the bookshelf, a basket of plastic apples in the dress-up center, and flash cards in a box by the circle-time carpet. To someone peeking in this room through a window it may *look* as though the children are *learning* about apples, but come on! *How much learning about apples can be going on if there isn't even an apple in the room?*

> Did you notice that this in-depth exploration of apples touched on every single developmental domain within DAP?

What senses are being developed with a fake plastic apple? What understanding deepened with a photocopied ditto of an apple to color? What language heard in the room where the children's experience of "apple" is limited to a flash card? Would you hear *juicy? sweet? red? seeds?* What kind of creativity is being nurtured when all the apples look the same? Would you hear lively descriptive language in a room where real, red, juicy, sticky, bruised apples with long stems and green leaves had been replaced by a three-by-five-inch flashcard that had the word *apple* written on it?

No way. Impossible. Children need experiences to attach words to.

We can no longer overlook the importance of early experiences. Nor can we ignore our responsibility of linking concept words to the playful learning experiences we provide in early childhood environments. Having the opportunity to engage in real, meaningful, hands-on experiences—as opposed to cute, fluffy time fillers, dittos, computer apps, and work sheets—is how children begin to unlock the secrets of their world. The experiences children crave are the very ones that allow them to construct a strong foundation that will support their learning.

As parents, educators, play-group leaders, teachers, grandparents, family child care providers, and administrators we must make time each day for children to create, move, sing, discuss, observe, and read all the while remembering that this foundation is held together by that which we call *play*. I wrote this book to share with you the reasons why.

PART 2

THE SEVEN THINGS

10

Make Time Each Day to . . . CREATE

ART IS NO longer done for art's sake. Instead, all the pieces of scribbled paper, the envelopes full of itty-bitty cuttings, the scores of easel paintings, the sticky holiday crafts, the #PinterestNails and #PinterestFails, as well as the result of yet another kiss good-bye accompanied by a sugary request to "Make a picture for Mommy today!" serve as proof that children *did something* today. Art projects have become the method by which parents are provided something tangible for the money they spend on child care fees and preschool tuition. In short, art has become a *receipt* for child care.

There are many reasons that this causes concern. First, what about the children who do not use art as their creative outlet? *It is important to realize that creating is not limited to the visual arts.* Many children enjoy painting and using watercolors, markers, glue, and other art materials. Some do not. These other children would often rather build with blocks, put puzzles together, or play dress-up in lieu of doing the day's art project. Yet, they are often coerced into "making something today." And, even worse, they are frequently interrupted while engaged in other creative outlets to come "do" whatever the teacher had planned for the day's project.

When children are basically forced to do art, the intrinsic value is lost. Some children are simply not interested in art projects! Instead, they build enormous block castles, make detailed and intricate

Legos creations, mold animated playdough sculptures, and prepare mud pies in the sandbox. They design maps and go hunting for treasures in the yard. They link together all hundred pieces of the train with a story and tale for each turn of the track. They direct the drama in the dress-up corner by monitoring the "lines" and "roles" played by each baby kitty and mama bear. These children are creating; it's just that *proof* of it often doesn't make it home.

My very first baby step in dealing with this situation was to get a classroom camera and start taking pictures. The pictures I took of the children engaged in both art and nonart activities were posted on the walls, tucked into envelopes and sent home, taped to doors, and contact papered onto the windows. It seemed to decrease the frequency of the "Where is their work?" "What did they make today?" and "Why doesn't my child paint?" questions. The communication strategy I'd like to offer at this juncture is to make sure you are focusing on what the child *is* doing, versus commenting excessively on what she's *not* doing. Example: it's not that she doesn't do art, it's that she DESIGNS AND CONSTRUCTS HUGE BLOCK TOWERS. This strategy might appear to be a matter of verbiage, but it really will make a huge difference in how dialogues play out!

Getting back to taking pictures, with the advent of digital and smartphone cameras we can take photos, print them, e-mail them, and text them to parents at home or at work. This sends a powerful message to the children and parents alike. It says that *all* creativity is valued and appreciated, not just the projects that can be displayed on a bulletin board. Plus, those pictures received earlier in the day might serve as a springboard to a good discussion at pickup time! You can use the pictures to start talking about what the child *did* do during the day, not what she *did not* do!

Photographs of various kinds of creative projects serve as visual documentation of the many things children enjoy doing while at preschool. Partnered with parent education, photographs serve as a helpful tool when talking about the "learning" that springboards off the open-ended, creative experiences you are providing.

My second cause for concern is when children *do* enjoy art but find their creative impulses stifled by grown-ups who are more worried about the carpet than the creative process. Here is another arena where teachers, directors, and parents go to battle. When so many people are working together, it is almost impossible to make everyone happy. Directors are caught between meeting the expectations of owners, administrators, teachers, and parents. Teachers sometimes must choose between doing exciting art projects and getting in trouble for children having red paint in their hair. Parents want their children to have fun experiences at school (often things they'd never permit at home!), yet don't want glue on the children's jeans. Teachers provide open-ended creative experiences but are questioned and challenged as to how the children are being "prepared" for kindergarten. Teachers might provide engaging sensorial experiences, such as ooblick and flubber, but are warned to watch out for the carpet. Splatter art and fingerpainting often get teachers in trouble because clothes get dirty.

Let's be honest for a minute, shall we? After a while, some of us give up because it is easier and less stressful to do brainless cookie-cutter art than it is to fight the fight. So we cut, and the children paste. We photocopy, the children color. But then when we get home we throw our hands up in frustration because (1) we are now doing what we claim to loathe, and (2) it appears as though some of the parents prefer it.

OK—STOP!

Take a deep breath . . . slow and easy, in and out. I could feel your pulse start to race and your blood begin to boil. Go make a cup of tea or get a cup of coffee, and sit back in a cozy chair. Calmer now? Good.

You need to ask yourself two very important questions and spend a minute or two really thinking about them before answering them honestly:

Question 1: WHO is tHe aRt FOR?

Is the art being done for the parents? school visitors? directors? administrators? owners? Or is it really *by* the children *for* the children?

Question 2: why is art being done?

To fit into the weekly theme? To fill up the bulletin board? To go home in the art file? To meet a portfolio requirement? To get a five on a rating scale? Or because the creative process is understood and honored?

I once observed a classroom of three-year-old children painting on glass jars for a holiday project. Most of the children used many colors and covered their entire jar. However, one child, Nick, made one big blue SPLAT on the side of his jar and announced that he was done! Later, during naptime, I cringed as I watched his teacher "finish" his jar.

While studying to become early childhood educators, we were all taught the importance of *process not product*. Yet how many of us actually stopped to think about what that really meant as we randomly selected art projects out of resource books to fill up our lesson plan book? Did we really understand the importance of *process* as we stapled twenty-four identical, cut-out, teacher-prepared, child-colored paper-plate owls to the bulletin board? Probably not.

The process of creating anything takes time. When cooking, you need time to read the recipe, shop for the ingredients, prepare the ingredients, and put everything together. Time is also necessary to actually cook or bake the meal. When time is limited, we do something quick and easy like microwave meals or take-out food. Although this faster process might relieve us of our hunger, it is not as enjoyable as a meal made when time is plentiful, savored, and shared with friends over a long drawn-out evening. The same is true with creative art experiences. When there is enough *time* and the *process* is appreciated, children can make one, two, three, even fifteen sponge paintings! The grown-ups should concentrate on facilitating a creative experience versus being narrowly focused on a final product with one eye locked on the clock, distracted by the ever-looming schedule.

So in one camp we have adequate time, appropriate materials, and teachers who value the process of being creative. By this we mean that the brushstrokes of red watercolor paint onto the paper are valued just as much as whatever the child might eventually announce he is making. The art you see on the walls is as varied as the children in the room. You might see various kinds of easel art, many collage projects, and many scribbled sheets taped or stapled to the walls. You will not see identical projects lining the bulletin boards. In fact, you might not see bulletin boards at all. (GASP!) Instead you might see children being given access to tape so they can display *their* work in *their* room at *their* height and eye level. You will see a celebration of individual creativity, not conformity to a set pattern or example. This room values process-oriented creativity.

Meanwhile, in the camp down the hall, there are tight, rigid schedules, limited materials, and a focus on the final product (what is being made) as the most important part of the creative process. In our "product-oriented camp" we see art that "looks like something," with everyone making *only one* identical construction paper spider, turtle, or cow. All the creations will be hung up on the bulletin board . . . together . . . in a line. If using clay or playdough, everyone will make a snake or snowman. If something new is introduced, you will hear, "Watch me, this is how we do it." You will not see individual expression, because the *product* is what is valued, not the *process* of how we got there. Therefore, to get the "correct" product, you will see lots of teacher-created examples and teacher-led activities. You will see children copying what the teacher demonstrated as the "right way to do it."

CREATIVE TIPS

Establishing a child-centered, process-oriented program can be very challenging and time consuming. However, this is our goal, so let's look at some things we need to remember as we begin the process:

CREATIVE TIP 1: EACH PROJECT WILL BE UNIQUE

This means that as you work on emphasizing process instead of product, you will no longer have bulletin boards covered with eighteen identical paper-plate animals and you saying, "But I let them glue the eyes wherever they wanted." Why? Because, again, the focus is on the process of creating, not having a set and determined finished product in mind. Want to do a gluing project? No problem! This time, though, instead of cutting out all the pieces and requiring or expecting the end result to "look like something," allow yourself to provide time, materials, and guidance and see what the children do with the glue, collage scraps, and construction paper you set out for them. Each child will create something different and unique. That is the beauty *and the purpose* of the creative process. It doesn't have to look like anything. Ever. Even if it's "fish week."

CREATIVE TIP 2: ART cannot Be FORCED

You cannot make children do art. Creativity flourishes when activities are done for enjoyment, not when they are forced or coerced. I forced someone once. It was just before Mother's Day back when I was still working at a program that "did holidays." The children were finishing up their Mother's Day projects, and the director of this particular school actually came in each room to make sure that each child had made something for Mama that would be presented at the Mother's Day Sunday brunch. In my room all of the children had made hot crayon melting cards, all of them—that is, except Patrick. Patrick just wasn't an art guy, and I was intent on not making him do something. My director came in and wanted to know why Patrick had not completed his project. I explained to her that he was really into Legos and that I had thought of an alternate idea for his present—I would take a picture of him building one of his Legos towers, and we could tape the photograph into a card for her. She looked at me over her thin, wire-rimmed glasses and insisted he make the same project as the other children. I resisted. She insisted. We went back and forth for a few days until I finally just said, "Forget it! You win!" I went over to Patrick and sat with him for a minute, watching as he intently built with his Legos before breaking two of my own rules: (1) I interrupted a child who was actively engaged, and (2) I was about to coerce a child into doing an art project.

"Patrick," I said, "we're making cards for our moms today. Come on over and make a crayon melting card for your mom." He looked at me, put his Legos down, stood up, and shuffled his feet over to the warming tray. He picked up a paper, grabbed a red crayon, and pounded three dots, bam! bam! bam! onto the paper. He lifted the paper off the warming tray and thrust it at me, saying, "Here, Ms. Lisa! I'm done!" before running back over to his Legos.

So much for a heart-felt emotionally charged project.

Later that month the crayon melting project was out again. This time Patrick was not in the block area building with Legos. He was pacing in front of the art table, stalking us, back and forth. He watched for *days* as the children melted crayons on different kinds of paper, but he never participated. Finally, one afternoon he called out, "Hey! Ms. Lisa! Are we making these for our moms?" I was silent for a minute, trying to wrap my brain around the context of his question. Then it dawned on me, the Mother's Day events of a few weeks past. "Patrick," I said, "you can make them for anybody you want."

INTERRUPTION! For the curious, I interrupt this anecdote to share with you insight into the personal evolution of how Lisa Murphy has conversations with children. If this same scenario played out now, I'd be more inclined to say something like, "You're wondering if you have to give them to someone."

He grabbed the next available chair and made about twenty of them! He used foil; he used wax paper; he used scratch paper and construction paper! He dropped a few little crayons into the warming tray and watched them slowly melt away in the heat. He made fast scribbles, big circles, and tiny ovals, and on the very last paper he wrote his name with a melting red crayon. Then, picking up all of his creations, he walked to his cubby and stuffed them in, announcing, "These! These are all for me!"

☺ creative tip 3:
THE SMALLER THE CHILD, THE BIGGER THE PAPER

Emphasizing the process means having HUGE sheets of paper available. Children need opportunities to be BIG before they can contain the small! Besides, even if you give them small paper, they will paint all over the table anyway! So provide big paper from the get-go. Butcher paper is awesome. I like fabric sheets too. What do I mean? I mean use old bed sheets in lieu of paper.

No toddler ever said, "BOY! I can't wait to bring this home and display it on the fridge!" Kids are into the process of it! Not the collection of it. So get sheets, let them paint BIG, then wash it out and do it again tomorrow!

No more dittos, patterns, and cut-out art. Instead, big sheets of paper for lots of open-ended art! Try butcher paper, art paper, newspaper, scratch paper, old desk calendars, copy paper, or even donated paper. For a while I didn't pay a dime for paper—I asked local businesses for donations. Here are some ways for you to possibly get free paper:

* Call the local newspaper, and ask if you can pick up the end rolls. End rolls are too small to use in the printing equipment but contain enough paper to last a classroom for a long time.

* Ask a local architectural firm if they will donate their recycled blueprints. The back of the blueprints is a large sheet of white paper, and the designed side is neat to look at too.

* Paint on newspaper. Adults like white paper; children don't care. Really.

* Ask your local office supply store if they will donate the dated desk calendars at the end of the year.

* Contact a local print shop to see if they generate an amount of scrap paper that is large enough for your use. Sometimes you can score huge sheets of cardstock when they are done with projects. Sometimes you can even get the cardstock end rolls! Keep your eyes peeled!

* Keep your eyes and ears open for your clients who work in companies that are changing letterhead designs, phone numbers, addresses, and so on. The paper is 8½" x 11", not really designed for art projects per se (too small), but excellent to have available for all the dramatic play writing that occurs each day! I was still living in San Diego County the year it was divided up from one area code to three. While this was expensive for business owners who had to keep changing letterhead, we preschool teachers made out like bandits!

After receiving any donated goods, be sure to send a thank-you note. Fill it with drawings from the children along with pint-sized handprints, and enclose some photos of the children using whatever the donated item(s) were. Not only is this good manners, it almost guarantees a repeat donation when you make another request.

creative Tip 4: Not Just paintbrushes anymore!

Focusing on the process of creating means seeing the possibility of painting with things other than paintbrushes. For example, try painting with any of the following:

* golf balls	* marbles	* kitchen brushes
* baby bottle brushes	* strawberry baskets	* squirt bottles
* toothbrushes	* plastic toy cars	* fingers
* noses	* Legos	* plungers
* bath puffs	* fish from the butcher	* magnets
* tennis balls	* dog toys	* spackle spreaders
* window squeegees	* flyswatters	* brooms
* trikes and bikes	* snails	* sponges

Provide big sheets of paper, and have some of the above-mentioned materials available. Add a few paper plates filled with bright, washable paint, and watch the creativity fly! Take some of this art outside so you don't have to worry about the walls and floor. Feeling brave? Do it inside! Remember to lay down sheets or drop cloths first. We aren't making a mess for the sake of making a mess—but we do realize that scattered stray splats might be reminders of an interesting project. Clean them up when you are all done. Better yet, give the kids a sponge and have them help!

CREATIVITY KILLERS

The Creative Spirit by Daniel Goleman, Paul Kaufman, and Michael Ray includes a list of "Creativity Killers" compiled by Teresa Amabile. I have taken the liberty of including a few of the Creativity Killers we might specifically find ourselves struggling with in our work with children, and have added some of my own commentary. Please note that "Creativity Killer 8: Baby Gap Syndrome" and "Creativity Killer 9: Dressing the Part" are both of my own creation and not affiliated with Amabile's work at all.

CREATIVITY KILLER 1: SURVEILLANCE AND HOVERING

When children are constantly under observation, their creative urges often go underground to hide. Think about this, if you are painting, perhaps drawing, maybe writing a new poem, would you want someone standing over you, watching every move, every sweep of the brush, and every stroke of the pen? Would you want them asking a lot of questions and commenting? Probably not. *Hovering gets in the way of the creative process.* Provide children with materials for creative expression, give them time to explore and use the materials, then back off.

I'd like to suggest having a place in the classroom or playroom where children can engage in "free flow art." In this place, materials such as colored glue, scissors, markers, crayons, recycled paper, masking tape, and hole punchers are available all the time. Short on space? Put the materials in a shoebox! Either way, call it the "creation station." It is a place where children can literally create whatever, whenever. In addition to many other art activities offered through the day, this center is "open daily" for creative exploration and imaginative play. What would need to happen for you to give this a go?

🎯 creativity Killer 2: Evaluation

When facilitating creative expression, we want to develop intrinsic motivation, not pressure to produce what others want, or what pleases teachers. Resist the urge to say, "What is it?" Resist the urge to really say anything about their creations.

If a child comes running to you saying, "*Look! Look! Look!*" Then do just that—look, look, look! The child did not say, "*Look, look, look, and please make a comment.*" If a child says, "Do you like my painting?" put the question back to her and say "Do you like *your* painting?"

I will often then turn the paper around or upside down and ask, "How about when I hold it this way? Or this way?" "Lie down, and tell me if you like it better when I hold it over you."

Practice this, say it with me: "How do *you* like your painting?" It's hard at first! But it's also a habit that can be learned. It is vital that you begin asking yourself, "Whose needs are being met by my comments?" Why do we feel the need to gush over each scribble? Each painting? Once while I was working as a mentor teacher in a preschool classroom, a little girl was creating truly lovely easel paintings. However, when she completed a picture, instead of announcing what a beautiful picture she was painting, or lavishing her with praise, or gushing over the colors she used, I simply asked her if she needed any more materials. She'd respond "yes" or "no" to my offerings of more paint or paper, and kept on working. Later in the day (she was still painting), her teacher came over to her and remarked about how lovely and beautiful her paintings were, and how she should be so proud, and, boy, her mom will be so pleased! Do you know what she did? She took the black paint and poured it all over the picture she was painting, turned away from the easel, and didn't paint anymore while I was there.

Cultivating intrinsic motivation becomes key as we encourage children to contemplate their own creations instead of paying so much attention to what others say or think about them.

As hard as it is, you must try with all your might to refrain from making evaluations and to practice *not* commenting. Remember that our actions really do speak louder than our words. YES! We want to be supportive! YES! We want to be encouraging! Years ago Bev Bos taught me (and many others) that the best way to show encouragement is by asking, "Do you need more paper?" What better way to show support and encouragement than by offering more of what they need to continue doing what they are doing?

⊚ creativity killer 3: overcontrol

Excessive micromanagement is frustrating for an adult and a child. Take the issue of children's names on their artwork. I have seen teachers go completely *berserk* because a child didn't want his name on the paper. When children acknowledge they are "done," I encourage teachers to ask, "Do you want your name on the paper?" If they say "yes," the teacher then asks, "Where do you want your name?" And then write it wherever the child indicates. If the child says, "I can write my own name," then give her the pen. If a child says, "I don't want my name on my paper," then leave it alone! We might inquire if they need help hanging it up to dry, or ask if they'd like some more paper, but that's it! There are no control battles over names on work, and *no one sneaks back to write it when the child isn't looking.* Children know their work and will keep it if they want it. And if they don't want it . . . so what? It's not yours to worry about. By being overly focused on making sure Jazmine's art gets into Jazmine's cubby, we are unintentionally contributing to the "receipt" mind-set!

I also discourage making models, samples, and examples for the children. This includes not drawing for children. When adults draw for children, children start to copy. If you currently draw for your children, remember, this is nothing more than a habit! When the time is right, you will work on breaking it. You can take a "baby step," and start by changing the hand you draw with. If you are left-handed, use your right, and vice versa. When sitting with the children, do not draw for them anymore. Simply copy what they have drawn using your nondominant hand. Eventually you want to work toward encouraging them to create independently without needing you right there to do it with them.

Independent creativity begins to emerge when you enhance the art area with colored paper, pens, markers, rulers, tape, glitter, colored pencils, and glue. Creativity flourishes when you continue to encourage their creations by asking, "Do you need anything else?" Be patient and gentle with yourself, and by all means give yourself time, but make sure you are working toward the goal of not drawing for them.

Copying the teacher is not art nor is it being creative; it is the regurgitation of someone else's idea. Instead of saying, "This [holding up example] is what we are all making today," try just putting the materials out for them to experience and explore! A morning spent squishing, molding, and poking clay does not have to turn into everyone bringing home an identical design! When adults overmanage children's art, it can lead to the children thinking that originality is a mistake (we are *all* making candy canes), and exploration is a waste of time (no, no, do it *this* way).

Rhoda Kellogg, child art expert and author of *Analyzing Children's Art*, reminds us that adults who encourage copy work and forbid or discourage spontaneous scribbling may harm the child's development in learning as well as in art. Her observations suggest that the child who has frequent opportunities to draw without a lot of adult interference learns faster and increases his cognitive ability more than he would if he were denied the opportunity.

I once saw a little poem hanging in the art area of a preschool classroom that I was visiting. It was back in the dark ages before smartphone cameras, and I didn't have any paper to copy it down, so I tried to remember it as best I could. It went something like this:

> When you
> Draw it for me
> Cut it for me
> Paste it for me
> Put it together for me
> All I learn is that you
> Do it better than me

I think this says it all.

If the children are painting with roller brushes and someone yells, "I need a flyswatter!" unless there really is a true, good, honest reason that you can't go get the flyswatter, go get the flyswatter! Telling the child "No," or "I can't right now," or "We aren't using flyswatters today," or "I'll get it tomorrow," when there is really no reason you can't just go get it right now, squashes creativity and stifles expression and exploration. But it lets you be the boss.

A frequent comment to this is, "But Lisa, if I get Tammy the flyswatter, *everyone* will want a flyswatter!" Or the infamous, "If I get something special for David, then they are *all* going to want something special!" SO WHAT? What is so wrong with that? What else on the day's agenda could be possibly more important than providing what they need in the here and now to deepen and extend this creative moment? Save NO for when you really need to say NO; it will retain its impact when it is used sparingly. When we say NO to children about things like flyswatters and roller brushes, it is because a part of us feels we need to be in charge! We feel the need to be in control. We worry that we are letting them get away with something, or that they will become spoiled or demanding because they are getting their way, but please, *please* hear me on this, we are not talking about a major ethical issue here, we are not addressing a moral dilemma, we are talking about a *paintbrush*! I would hope this is not the hill you want to die on.

I teach teachers, parents, and workshop participants to begin saying YES as often as possible. It's not YES because you are letting them get away with something. It's YES because YES keeps things moving, which deepens explorations, which supports innovative thinking and problem solving.

As I mentioned previously, I have recently discovered the phrase, "What part of this can I say *yes* to?" I have learned that this simple phrase assists adults in taking an oft-needed step away from having to be the boss of everything.

When I was an acting student in Chicago, a large part of the training consisted of doing improv scenes, where our teacher would give us a few descriptions about the situation, and we were left to perform the scene for the class. When improvising dialogue, we would often ask questions to keep the energy moving forward and to keep the scene alive. When we asked questions of our fellow players and they said, "YES," "SURE," or "OK," the scene stayed alive and kept moving, kept progressing. The minute a player said, "NO," "NOT YET," or "NOT RIGHT NOW," it would die. One person was trying to move forward while someone was stopping it dead in its tracks.

Working with children is no different. The children are throwing out questions and requests. Our answers determine the length, intensity, and power of the scene that gets played out. Use that power *with* and *for* the children, not over them. Say *yes* as often as possible. *Go get the flyswatter!*

creativity killer 5: pressure

Lofty, inappropriate expectations of a child cause unnecessary pressure and can lead to frustration for both adult and child. When children are expected to "make a picture for mommy" and, on top of that, make a picture that "looks like something" when they are still in the scribble scrabble stage of creating and drawing, the child is pressured to perform above his years and ability.

Rhoda Kellogg identified twenty basic scribbles that serve as the starting point not only for childhood artistic creativity but for writing as well. From making basic, random scribbles on a piece of paper, the child will move on to placing these scribbles in different, yet consistent places on their paper. From here, they will make shapes, then move on to combining shapes. We see the creation of suns, humans, and then flowers. Eventually we will see rainbows, buildings, and houses, and then transportation objects, like cars and trucks. Things that "look like something" cannot be created until the children have had the time and experience of drawing (over and over again) the lines, shapes, squiggles, and scribbles they will need in order to put these things together on their paper! Houses and people are combinations of shapes. Shapes are combinations of lines and scribbles. It is only *after* being allowed to cycle through these universal stages that they combine all of their skills to make pictures containing what we call "representational art," meaning "something that looks like something."

Examples of Rhoda Kellogg's stages of scribbling have been included at the end of the chapter for your review and reference. As you look at the examples, you can see how one leads to the next. We must try our best not to force children to make humans if they are still making dots. We must not suggest suns if they are still making roving lines. We must debunk the belief that child art is worthless unless it looks like something! We must realize that self-taught scribbles, lines, dots, and circles constitute the beginning elements of artistic creativity (and writing!). We must learn to be patient and allow children to proceed through the many stages of scribbling without a lot of undue comments and pressure.

creativity killer 6: lack of time

Children need lots and lots of free time to savor and explore an activity. We posted a sign on the door of one of my classrooms that said, "This is a child's place, and we move at a child's pace." I was honored sometime later when a school in Indiana posted the same sign in their front entry hall! Child time is totally different than grown-up time! When children are interrupted and torn out of deep concentration, their innate desire to work through something is compromised. Statements such as, "Hurry up!" "Time to go!" and "Come over here and do something else!" deprive children of the chance to stay with an activity and see it through. Permitting a beginning, a middle, and an end to a play session is very important. If always pressured to "Hurry and clean up" prior to the play being done, the child is essentially never given time to finish. He loses interest in even *starting* anything because the pattern has been set that there is never enough time to bring it to a natural close. Pretty soon you have a classroom filled with bored children who have been given a strong message, whether spoken or implied, that their interests take a backseat to clocks and schedules.

Children need time to get involved with things that interest them. I have seen a lot of curricula that are a mile wide and an inch deep. On the surface it looks like the children are covering so much ground, but there is no time to absorb anything. There's no depth. It brings up images of tourists on vacation with strict sightseeing agendas! Hurry, hurry! Go here, go there, take a selfie, post it, take a video, no time to stop and really absorb the experience, because we have to catch the train by 4:45.

Making time is crucial as we start paying attention to cultivating creativity.

⊚⊚ Creativity Killer 7: Measurable Outcomes = Funding

Ask any teacher what's the first thing to get cut from a budget: art, drama, music. Even when content standards exist for the arts, teachers will tell you it doesn't matter, because the only thing anyone cares about are the subjects that are tested. With our culture's overemphasis on testing, the arts are often pushed out or given a once-a-month-special-treat-Friday-afternoon time slot, their importance being given lip service only.

Since the first edition of this book was completed, we've watched the United States adopt state standards, then No Child Left Behind (NCLB), then Race to the Top (RTTT), and now many states have adopted Common Core. Consistent throughout? Overemphasis on language/literacy and math and an absence of the other subject areas, including the arts.

With science standards and testing criteria looming on the horizon, we've seen a push for activities that encourage science, technology, engineering, and math (STEM). Many are saying "Turn STEM into STEAM!" by adding art in there too, which is awesome, and I admire their efforts. I just think it's a pity that art and creativity must be escorted in the side door on science's guest list and not allowed in for its own sake.

We still have a lot of work to do.

◉ CReativity KiLLeR 8: BaBy GaP SYNDROME

"Dealing with Baby Gap Syndrome" is the title of an article I wrote awhile back. There are many faces to Baby Gap Syndrome (BGS). Permit me to elaborate: meet "Little Man." Little Man suffers from BGS. He comes to school dressed in his designer shorts and matching shirt. His shirt remains tucked in all day, and he even wears a belt. His hair is slicked back with gel; he looks good, he smells good! Little Man changes his shirt after lunch. His sneakers remain clean day in and day out, and he always looks as neat as a pin. He also, however, does absolutely nothing all day for fear of getting messy or dirty. When he does choose to play with the playdough, he washes his hands every five minutes. Little Man cries if he gets a little bit of paint on his shirt and has an emotional breakdown on the playground when he gets mud on his pants.

Then there is Little Miss. Little Miss also suffers from BGS. Little Miss dresses better than any of her teachers. Little Miss has shoes that match her Little Miss purse; she has never been seen in jeans. Little Miss often comes to school wearing party dresses that cost more than her teacher's weekly paychecks. Little Miss has a clear vision of where the bow in her hair needs to be. Like our Little Man, Little Miss tends not to be very active during the day, because her clothing prevents it. When she does roll up her taffeta and get into the ooblick, she will often end up in tears, asking you to please "throw this away so Mama won't get mad." At some point during the year, Little Miss will bound into school announcing that she isn't allowed to paint anymore because it "ruins my clothes."

Don't you wish you had a dollar for every time you said, "Please send your child to school in clothes you don't care about!" We can encourage, demand, threaten, bribe, write notes home, scream, post signs, and tell parents until we are blue in the face about the importance of wearing "play clothes" to school, but to no avail! It is frustrating to feel like our words are ignored, and even more so when, after all our efforts and insistence, the children still come to school suffering from BGS.

I have seen children proudly drag their parents out onto the yard to show off the tree forts, castles, and mud houses they spent all day building and creating, designing and painting only to be asked, "Why are you so dirty?" and be informed with heavy sighs, "There's paint on your new shoes."

It makes me want to scream! What message is sent when there is so much emphasis on clothing and footwear at the expense of playing and exploring? Can the shirt really be more important than the opportunity to engage in a new creative experience? If it is, then it is a shirt that does not belong in preschool. I actually had a child come to school once wearing a green, crushed silk flower-girl dress, and on her feet were tap shoes! I looked at Mama, who smiled, shrugged her shoulders, and said, "Well, that's what she wanted to wear! Have a good day!" Then she turned and bounced out the door. Sure, her daughter wanted to wear it, but who would get yelled at if it got covered in ooblick, flubber, or easel paint?

Before I continue, though, I want to stand up and tip my hat with gratitude to the parents who do realize the importance of play clothes. A big thank-you to the parents who don't worry about whether the shirts and shorts "match" but care more about their children having a fun, exciting day. Hats off to the parents who might still choose to dress their children in designer clothes but don't get hung up and bent out of shape when the logos and labels get muddy. We are able to watch your children run around and play without observing the hesitation that is so often apparent in children who have not been given this little bit of freedom.

During program orientation and back-to-school nights, I tell all the families, "Send them in clothes you don't care about!" I then show pictures of the children in action, and they immediately understand! I met a director who tells parents, "If your child doesn't get dirty at school, then we aren't doing our job!" Another friend who provides family child care tells all her new clients, "I guarantee I will ruin their clothes!" And a colleague who teaches preschool tells her families, "If you want the children to be able to wear it in public again, don't let them wear it here!" Sound too harsh?

Too firm? Maybe. But sometimes our words need to be firm so they understand that we are serious!

The reason I like to show parents pictures is so they can see firsthand what the children are doing and begin to understand the creative process! I have discovered that parents sometimes have a misconception that their children are getting dirty because teachers are not paying attention. PowerPoints, short video clips, and photographs are tools for educating parents not only about the creative process but also about your involvement and investment in the activity as well.

In addition, through parent workshops, parent meetings, articles about hands-on, creative messy play, a back-to-school orientation, well-written contracts, and parent handbooks, you can begin to battle BGS. Educators and providers need to be able to verbalize why creative art and other kinds of messy play are important. We must be able to identify the skills that are being developed as children engage in these hands-on experiences. Remember that the parents aren't there during the day to see the creativity, cooperation, and process firsthand; all they might see is the red paint in the hair and the glue on the jeans.

In our programs children are not required to wear smocks, but we do use washable paint for all projects. At orientation, parents are informed of the high level of creativity we encourage, so they are asked to keep lots of extra clothes in their child's cubby. Understanding that lots of extras can be taxing for some families, there is also a big tub of community clothes I have accumulated over the years at garage sales and consignment shops that children can borrow from if necessary. I refuse to let clothing be that which hinders a child's creativity.

◉ creativity Killer 9: Dressing the Part

And finally, please please please make sure you are dressing the part too! One of the saddest things I've ever seen was a child running to welcome her teacher back after an absence: the teacher backed away from her small, painty hands, saying sternly, "Don't touch me."

Just as we fight the good fight for children to come to school dressed in play clothes, you too must dress for creative play. Save the fancy clothes, the nightclub clothes, and the designer clothes for locations where they are appropriate, not the preschool. Go buy three pairs of pants you don't care about and a whole bunch of shirts from the Goodwill. I think overalls are the best for preschool teachers—all those pockets come in handy for tape, scissors, band-aids, markers, tissues, and whatever. No one is there for a fashion contest; we are there to be with children.

Regardless of how "into" your teaching you are, if you are over-dressed, you are going to be worried about your clothes. Dressy clothes have no place in an early childhood environment. Now maybe you are the office receptionist—by all means, dress up if you would like! But let us not make the mistake of forgetting that what goes on in the front office is much different than what is happening in the art area, sandbox, and playground! Different jobs, different needs. If you are dressed in clothes that you are worried about, you will shy away from engaging interactions and explorations. If you back away from the art table for fear of "getting dirty," guess what the children in your class are going to do?

The topic of dress codes comes up frequently in professional circles. Many pages of employee handbooks are used to define, regulate, and otherwise enforce the attire of the staff. No this, no that, no jeans, no overalls, no shorts, no T-shirts (except on Fridays), more no no no no no's. I expect staff to be clean, fresh smelling, and dressed, meaning body parts covered, no boobs or butts hanging out. Other than that, my rule is as follows: clothes, accessories, shoes, hair, nails, and jewelry should not interfere with your interactions with the children.

I have seen teachers who do just fine with long acrylic nails and some who can no longer zip zippers open a thermos, change a diaper, or tie shoes. I might need to inform the teacher who is no longer able to function that it might be best for her to remove her acrylic nails. I would *not*, however, create a policy, circulate a memo, create a new rule, or otherwise require all teachers to remove their long, pretty, brightly painted nails simply out of superficial "fairness."

It would be inappropriate for me to have one-size-fits-all policies for my teachers, just as I resist one-size-fits-all policies for children. We deal with things as they come up. We do not enforce generalizations in order to ease management duties or responsibilities. If someone needs a meeting about not covering all their parts or wearing too much perfume, sit them down and talk with them. We are losing our ability to communicate. We have become fearful of conflict, so to keep things "nice," and in the name of fairness, we establish knee-jerk policies that are not fair to anyone.

One of my former employees used to wear tall, wedge sandals that were so high they would make your nose bleed. I did not "not allow" her to wear her big shoes simply because she "might" trip. If, however, they had inhibited her running, jumping, or otherwise interacting with the children, that would have been another story, and we would have dealt with it at that time. She is an amazing teacher. And guess what? Her shoes did not change her amazingness! I am usually in jeans. Am I "less professional" than a counterpart who might wear a suit? If we put Laminated Lady in heels and a dress, would she all of a sudden become a better teacher?

Please know that I am aware of and respect the fact that certain religious belief systems dictate and regulate the clothing worn by their members. These religious requirements and choices are not what I am talking about here. What I am being faced with lately are recent mandates that providers and teachers in infant, toddler, and preschool classrooms wear khaki pants, collared shirts, ties, heels, skirts, and nylons.

I ask, "Why?" They say, "Professionalism!" Yet I wonder aloud how folks who are barely paid a livable wage are expected to spend such a large percentage of their money on clothing! I wonder if their organizations are now providing a clothing allowance for required items. Are they reimbursed for dry cleaning? But mostly, *I wonder if it is a way of cleverly circumventing the necessity of providing meaningful, creative, messy, artistic, child-centered play.*

I think it goes much deeper than what we see on the surface. Like most things, there is a larger issue. It's not that they don't want you in jeans. It's that we look more like a "teacher" when we are wearing something else. Like a tie and pressed pants. Yet do I stop being a teacher if I'm in clean overalls, a nice T-shirt, and sneakers? I was at a post-workshop dinner break with a group in Indiana, and the waitress asked what we were in town for. "Teacher training!" we enthusiastically replied. "What grade?" she asked. "Preschool!" "Oh . . ." she said, "So you're not really teachers . . . " I looked at our waitress and then looked around the table. Who did I see? A family child care provider of fifteen years, a former preschool teacher, now program director, myself, and a woman who has a PhD and teaches child development at the local college. But somehow we are not really "teachers" because we work with young children. So I guess the logic goes that if we aren't really teachers because we work with young children, and we are only really teachers if we teach a "grade," then if we dress and look the way the grade school teachers do, then we can be considered teachers. Is that it?

I am told that these clothing requirements are designed to promote professionalism, thus encouraging parents to treat the teachers with respect. Yes, it is true that folks dressed up for a night on the town will get a nicer table, possibly faster seating, and more than likely better service. If you have a nice car (and it's washed), it will get staged when you use valet parking. And I doubt that anyone would question the authority of a red power tie. But we are talking about folks who are working with babies! With toddlers! How can you dart after a runaway preschooler if you are in heels? Teachers need to be able to move around, clean up spills, change diapers, be burped on, be thrown up on, run after children, roll on the floor, play in the mud and water, and provide creative art experiences every day. Dress codes and clothing requirements MUST take these things into consideration!

You do not become professional by wearing certain clothes. Respect for the self translates into respect for others. Pride and professionalism come from within. If a teacher really is a "professional," her "professionalism" will present itself daily during interactions with colleagues, parents, directors, and children whether they are in jeans, a skirt, coat and tie, sneakers, or high heels.

Furthermore, *if we think we can create good teachers with "nice" clothes, does it not follow that we disguise bad teaching with the same?*

"Sit down! Be quiet!" "Stop that! I will call your mother!" "Don't make me come over there! No! No! No!" But *DAMN* she looks good!

I guarantee that when you are presented the opportunity to observe true professionals, you will be able to identify them by their love and laughter, their dedication to their career, and their passion and commitment to the children regardless of what they are wearing.

Twenty Basic Scribbles

Back in the late 1960s, a researcher named Rhoda Kellogg performed extensive investigations about how children's writing develops over time. She found that a child's scribbles evolve in some sort of sequence from simple dots and lines to more complex designs. Kellogg's research identified twenty basic scribbles:

SCRIBBLE 1: dot

SCRIBBLE 2: single vertical line

SCRIBBLE 3: single horizontal line

SCRIBBLE 4: single diagonal line

SCRIBBLE 5: single curved line

 SCRIBBLE 6: multiple vertical line

 SCRIBBLE 7: multiple horizontal line

 SCRIBBLE 8: multiple diagonal line

 SCRIBBLE 9: multiple curved line

 SCRIBBLE 10: roving open line

 SCRIBBLE 11: roving enclosing line

 SCRIBBLE 12: zigzag or waving line

 SCRIBBLE 13: single loop line

 SCRIBBLE 14: multiple loop line

 SCRIBBLE 15: spiral line

SCRiBBLe 16: multiple-line overlaid circle

 SCRiBBLe 17: multiple-line circumference circle

 SCRiBBLe 18: circular line spread out

 SCRiBBLe 19: single crossed circle

 SCRiBBLe 20: imperfect circle

Following experimentation with the basic scribbles, children will begin to link what they know, create new shapes and new designs, and will proceed through the following stages prior to creating representational art and prior to writing:

 implied diagrams and shapes

 crosses

 combinations using two shapes

 aggregates (three or more shapes)

mandalas (dividing space into equal parts)

 suns

 radials

 suns with faces

 humanoids

 humans

THE IMPORTANCE OF CREATING: A REVIEW

1. Watch out for Creativity Killers.

2. Creating is NOT limited to visual arts.

3. Be aware of the stages of scribbling.

4. Realize the importance of process, not product.

5. Make sure there is enough time for creative exploration.

6. Creative play can be messy play, so dress accordingly.

some THiNGS to THiNK ABOUt

1. How do I make time for creating in school?

2. How do I make time for creating in my own life?

3. In what area(s) am I creative?

4. Have I, up until now, viewed "creativity" as being limited to the visual arts?

5. Are there children in my class who are more "nonart" creative?

6. What might they need from me to continue this level/style of creativity?

7. How can I make the environment more welcoming for them?

8. Does my school suffer from Baby Gap Syndrome?

9. Can we make a small step toward dealing with Baby Gap Syndrome?

10. Do we need to revisit how the teachers are dressing the part?

11. Which of the Creativity Killers do I struggle with most? Why?

12. What can I begin to do about these Creativity Killers?

13. Which one of the Creativity Killers do I struggle with least? Why?

14. How does making time each day to CREATE meet a child's cognitive, language/literacy, social/emotional, and physical developmental needs?

15. What steps can I take to be more confident when pointing out these developmental connections to parents? colleagues? naysayers?

16. What is one thing I can do Monday to begin making time each day to create?

✎ NOTABLE AND QUOTABLE

Art is the language of the heart.

—Margaret Mead, anthropologist (attributed)

The only education worth having is an art education.

—Abraham Maslow (attributed)

You can run an art program for an entire year for what it costs to buy a computer.

—Rena Upitil, in *The Child and the Machine* by Alison Armstrong and Charles Casement

Learning to think creatively in one discipline opens the door to understanding creative thinking in all disciplines. Educating this universal imagination is the key to producing lifelong learners.

—Robert and Michèle Root-Bernstein, *Sparks of Genius*

Imagination is more important than knowledge.

—Albert Einstein

11

Make Time Each Day to . . . MOVE

CAN YOU REMEMBER the *feel* of hopscotch, leapfrog, cartwheels, piggyback, playing ball, turning somersaults, splashing in puddles, climbing trees, riding bikes, twirling until you fell down dizzy, hopping on pogo sticks, leaping off of swings, spinning hula hoops, jumping rope, and playing tag, Ring Around the Rosie, Red Rover, and kickball? And where were you when you engaged in such active play? Many of us found freedom of movement when we were outside, where we were often left to our own devises to run ourselves silly.

Open any book on child development, and you will read about the connection between brain development and physical movement. (DAP dedicates a whole domain to it!) In his book *Brain Rules*, author John Medina reminds us that as humans we are designed to be in motion. Although children develop many skills in tandem with each other, from our knowledge of physical development and from the work of Carla Hannaford, who wrote *Smart Moves: Why Learning Is Not All in Your Head*, we know that they grow from the neck down and from the trunk out. This means the large, gross-motor muscles of arms and legs need to be developed and strengthened before the fine-motor muscles of hands and fingers. Large-motor activities such as climbing, jumping, running, and spinning come *before* small-motor activities like holding pens and pencils, tying shoes, and zipping zippers.

The challenge in making time each day for moving is not to *prove* that children need to be physically active. Our challenge is that too many people believe the other domains within developmentally appropriate practice are more important than large- and small-motor development. They are not.

The outdoors is more conducive to the active learning style of young children, yet we still read about schools eliminating recess. Why? The reasons usually consist of some version of the following:

* fear of lawsuits over playground injuries

* the sudden (yet questionable) increase of "unsavory" adults lurking nearby

* a shortage of adults willing to supervise the playground

* pressure to increase academic performance

* testing frenzy

The recess crisis came to a head in the late 1990s. Popular news stories included an elementary school in Virginia that did not have recess; rather it had a "Walk 'n' Talk" program where, after lunch, children were allowed to walk around four orange cones that were set up in the yard. Although it was considered "social time," the children had to keep their voices down and all walk in the same direction. Three years later, after a protest led by local parent Rebecca Lamphere (who has since been referred to as the "Erin Brockovich of the swing set"), not only was recess mandated by the district but by the state as well.

Around this same time, the superintendent of schools in Atlanta, Georgia, was quoted as saying, "We are intent on improving academic performance. You don't do that by having kids hanging on the monkey bars." While Virginia was mandating recess, Georgia was taking it away. Atlanta was one of the first school districts to eliminate recess, going so far as to build new elementary schools without playgrounds. And while recess has since been reinstated in Atlanta, in part due to the work of parents such as Lamphere and recess experts such as Olga Jarrett, the complaint now is that there is no place to go! The late 1990s found many school administrators caving in to the pressure of raising test scores by doing something symbolic—they eliminated what is often considered the most expendable part of the day, recess.

Ideally, of course, every school board member, administrator, and politician who approves such outlandish doctrine as eliminating recess from preschools in the name of "readiness" and from elementary schools for "higher test scores" should be required to teach these children . . . for a week . . . when it's raining. I will then inquire as to whether recess is still viewed as an "expendable" waste of time.

The actual percentage of how many schools in the United States have eliminated recess varies anywhere from 20 percent to 40 percent depending on whose website you are visiting. Either way, it's not 0 percent, and that should cause alarm in even the most uninvolved person. Why? Because eliminating recess does not eliminate a child's need to move around. When children are deprived of places where they *can* engage in developmentally appropriate, large-motor, physical feats, they will start doing them in the classroom. And just because it is developmentally appropriate for children to jump, run, and climb, doesn't mean it's OK for that to happen on the table, on the bookshelf, or in the library. When children have limited access to outdoor places and are kept inside too long, they begin to exhibit behaviors that are treated as *behavior* problems, even though they are not. They are actually *expectation* problems.

TODAY'S SPECIALS: LABELS DU JOUR AND ACRONYMS à LA MODE

Recess provides a welcomed change of pace, time away from formal lessons, and the ability to socialize and relax. After a vigorous playtime, students return to their classroom better able to concentrate. Why then are we still seeking to eliminate recess? What happens when it's gone? Let's take a peek:

* Preschoolers with limited outside time begin to run and shout in the classroom; elementary students wiggle in their desks, unable to focus on the lesson at hand. This happens day in and day out.

* Children are told to "Sit still! Sit still!" "Pay attention!" "Eyes on me!" "Focus!" "Stop moving around!"

* Finally, the breaking point is reached: "You know, I'm *tired* of telling you to sit still!" says the teacher. "You need an assessment!"

* The child is now shuffled from classroom, to principal's office, to doctor, where she is given an assessment, an evaluation, an Individualized Education Plan (IEP), a diagnosis, and, all too frequently, a prescription.

* Our out-of-control child is given medication that will "assist" her in focusing, keeping still, and paying attention. The magic medicine will make the child easier to control (oops, I mean "handle"), thus making the teacher's day run a little smoother.

We are quick to write a prescription and dispense medications when children are not sitting still and paying attention, but dare I propose that maybe the problem is not with the children but perhaps with the *information she is being demanded to pay attention to. Is it even worth listening to and sitting still for?*

It is my experience that many so-called hyper kids are really crying out for someone to pay attention to them and provide projects, assignments, activities, and experiences that are meaningful and relevant. And they need to *move!* They need to get up, move around, touch things, and be fully engrossed in activities, not passively sitting at tables and in desks *watching.* They need to be *doing.* I worry that, for whatever reason, rather than figuring out what these children need from us and from their classrooms, we simply stuff them full of medication to make them more manageable.

The *Diagnostic and Statistical Manual of Mental Disorders* (DSM-5) is now in its fifth edition. It is the psychological reference tool used for diagnosing and classifying disorders. Although first and foremost used by clinical practitioners, it can serve as a practical, functional resource for teachers who benefit from having a common language when discussing and learning more about the various diagnoses that some of our children have been given.

Now, please remember, that as an educator you have the ability (and *right*) to access the information contained within the *DSM-5* for professional and personal reference, but you *do not* have the right to make a diagnosis. You can get in a lot of trouble if you do. And *that* being said, I am not making a position statement on the topic of *diagnosis* within this book at all. The point I wish to make is that in previous editions of the *DSM*, two diagnoses that parents and teachers came face to face with on a regular basis were attention deficit disorder (ADD) and attention deficit hyperactivity disorder (ADHD). In past editions of the *DSM*, they were two separate diagnoses. In the revised *DSM-5*, they are not; they are now a single diagnosis. If you are a clinician, there are various new diagnostic criteria changes that I am sure you are well aware of, but for my teacher and parent readers, I think it is important for you to be aware that the two have become one, the diagnosis is now Attention-Deficit/Hyperactivity Disorder, and the *term* would now be ADHD.

Copies of the *DSM-5*, and therefore the diagnostic criteria for ADHD and other disorders, are readily available online and in your local library. A simple cursory glance at the diagnostic criteria would lead even a minimally active, fidgety person to succumb to self-diagnosis! I have a hard time sitting still, but I have learned ways to focus and pay attention. I have had to learn how to stay on task. I have had to figure out a way to keep active outside of these situations so that when I must sit and pay attention, I am able to do so. I am able to sit for lectures and classes, because I know that I am going to get a break. I can focus on their message and their assignments because I know that I will be given time to get up, move around, walk around campus, and burn off some steam. *I can focus on what needs to be done because I know at some point I am going to be able to get up and move around* . . . and even if I don't, I am an adult, I can self-regulate. If I need to, I will quietly remove myself from the situation and go take a break.

But what happens when you are little and don't yet have the language capacity to express yourself in such a manner? What happens when you are older and can, but are denied?

When children are not provided with an appropriate place to run around and move, the behaviors that are typically reserved for the playground begin to make their way into the classroom! All of a sudden we have this influx of "hyper" children. Are they really hyper, or are they having inappropriate expectations placed on them? Our children are being medicated because they can't sit still long enough to complete a stack of dittos. Well, that's just plain ludicrous. We are missing the forest for the trees here! The problem is not with the child; the problem is with adult expectations of the child. It is not *wrong* that the child can't complete the stack of dittos. It is wrong that we are expecting him to do it in the first place.

Carla Hannaford tells us that the causal agents of ADHD have always included environmental factors such as developmentally inappropriate curriculum, rigid educational systems, lack of body movement, too much screen time, as well as a lack of creative play. In his book *The Myth of the A.D.D. Child*, Dr. Thomas Armstrong says that attention disorders in general have been referred to by some as recent historical developments invented in cognitive psychology laboratories and given life by the American Psychiatric Association, the U.S. Department of Education, and the chemical laboratories of our pharmaceutical corporations. Big pharma is a multibillion-dollar enterprise.

I am not a doctor. All I am saying is to investigate all options and do your homework before allowing someone to put a child in your care or classroom on medication. Just because a child is loud and active doesn't mean she requires a diagnosis! Although the title is dated in regard to the new *DSM* criteria, *The Myth of the A.D.D. Child* by Armstrong is still a valuable resource as it provides fifty non-medicinal ways of dealing with many of the potentially challenging behaviors you might be observing without falling into the "She needs Ritalin!" trap.

HOW ABOUT THOSE LEARNING STYLES?

It helps everyone in the room when parents and providers take some time to brush up on their knowledge of learning styles:

- ✿ **Visual learners** prefer to take in information through their eyes (seeing).

- ✿ **Auditory learners** prefer processing new information via their ears (listening).

- ✿ **Kinesthetic learners** prefer hands-on learning (touching and moving).

It is the kinesthetic learners who are often incorrectly labeled as having ADHD, not because they are "bad kids," but because most educational environments (child care centers included) do not make room, literally or physically, for them.

It is in our best interest (and our children's) to have a general understanding of the three basic learning styles listed above. Why? (Please let me repeat myself.) Because many children labeled as hyper and subsequently put on medication do *not* have ADHD, they are kinesthetic learners! They learn through their bodies! They touch everything and move around a lot because they organize information through their bodies.

Now I must interrupt with a quick explanation here—*everyone uses all three learning styles.* Everyone is visual, auditory, *and* kinesthetic. When you are reading the paper, you are tapping into your visual skills. When listening to a song on your MP3 player, your auditory skills kick in. And when opening a jar of peanut butter, you are using your kinesthetic abilities. Understand what I mean?

What you also have is a *preference* for how you take in information. Please, please, please do not think "Oh well, I'm visual so I can't listen when teacher is talking," or "I'm auditory, I can't write the essay." No no no no labeling! No "excusing." Instead, find understanding. It is this *understanding* that will assist us, especially when working with children who have a kinesthetic preference and want to stand up for circle time or when they are eating snack, and we wish they would just sit down for cryin' out loud!

Visual learners organize information through their eyes. During story time these children are clamoring to be right in front of you so they can see the pictures, yet they still holler out, "I can't see! I can't see!" Children with a visual preference notice your first gray hair, your new purple toenail polish, your shiny new red car, and even the zit that sprouted on your chin overnight. They love to read and write. They enjoy experimenting with inventive spelling. They like to use sidewalk chalk to write stories. They are list makers and need to write everything down. As they get older, visual learners would rather you text them or send an e-mail than call.

Auditory learners don't need to write it down. (As they get older, they will record the professor's lecture and listen to it in the car.) They take in new information through their ears. During circle time, they don't need or want to be on the carpet; they are in the block center, the sandbox, or painting at an easel. But what are they still doing? That's right. They are still listening! These children are not the "One, two, three! Your eyes on me" types; their *ears* are on you instead! They like to listen to music, they tend to be chatty, and they really enjoy talking on the phone. As they get older, they might do their homework with earbuds tucked in their heads, much to the dismay and frustration of the *visual* parent! "Take those things out! How can you concentrate!? They are so distracting!" Distracting to whom, though—the child or the adult?

Kinesthetic learners prefer *acting out* the story, not listening to it; *doing* the science experiment, not watching it; and *building* the model airplane, not looking at pictures of it in a book. They have to be up and moving. During group time, these are the children who are standing in the back (you want them to sit); they are asking you questions (you want them to be quiet); they are touching every-thing in sight (you want them to be still). You know who I'm talking about!

Now, if you had a room full of visual learners, would you put blindfolds on them? Of course not. Would you put cotton in the ears of an auditory learner? No way. Yet every time we tell the kines-thetic child to "sit still and be quiet!" we are essentially putting on a blindfold and stuffing their ears. I am not going to lie to you—it is easier to meet the needs of a visual or an auditory learner. But after twenty-plus years in the field, I am not after easy, I'm after meaningful. It is harder to identify what the kinesthetic children might need to feel reflected in the classroom. But that's our job, and we need to figure it out. And honestly, if this is too much of a burden for the adult in the room, maybe THAT is who needs an adjustment— not the child.

I heard about a very creative teacher who, instead of demanding assessments, gathered up a few milk crates and filled them with big, thick, heavy college textbooks. Then, when one of the children started getting antsy she would say, "Hey! Mr. Jones needs his books back. Please bring them to him."

With that simple comment, out goes the child, out go the books, and out goes the milk crate! After laboriously dragging the heavy crate down the hall, the child would arrive at Mr. Jones's room. Then *he* would say, "Thanks so much! How did you know I needed them? [smile] Wait now, since you're here, why don't you bring Mrs. Smith hers back as well." And with a nod to the corner, a second milk crate filled with even more books would be dragged back down the hall.

A fifteen-minute (if even that long) break from assignments, desks, tables, and chairs and probably enough energy exerted allowed the child to come back and stay focused on the task at hand. Maybe not as "easy" as medications but definitely more meaningful.

So which learning style preference works best within our current, traditional, educational model? Which one does not? Which child will be sent to the office for being disruptive? Which one will receive notes sent home for not paying attention in class? Who will be accused of not being on task? Who could be mistakenly labeled as having an attention disorder?

I am concerned with the haste in which we are diagnosing, labeling, prescribing, and medicating children. Many of the children who are said to have ADHD suffer from what Armstrong refers to as "disappearing symptom syndrome." Amazingly enough, their "hyperness" decreases in classrooms with engaging, interactive, supportive teachers but suddenly "appears" again when in rigid, overcontrolling environments. Then, like magic, their symptoms disappear again when back in the engaging classroom! Not surprisingly symptoms usually disappear completely when in gym class, on the football field, or while running the track. Hmmmm.

If these children truly had an organic impairment, common sense tells us that they would be displaying their symptoms all the time, not just in certain situations. If you have heart disease, you have heart disease wherever you go. If you have the flu, you have it wherever you go, not just when you are in Laminated Lady's classroom.

My personal experience is that when these "hyper" children are offered adequate outdoor playtime in addition to meaningful and interesting experiences in their indoor environments, their symptoms disappear. I am reminded of a time when I was asked by a preschool teacher to come and observe one of her students. Upon my arrival I spoke with the director and the teacher, received some input, and then spent the morning watching the child interact with the environment, the materials, the teacher, and the other students. We spent some time inside and then moved out onto the yard. As we were observing the children on the bikes, playing with sand and shovels, climbing ladders, swinging, and sliding, I inquired as to what the teacher's concerns were regarding the child's behavior on the playground. "Outside?" she said, "Oh, he's fine outside."

Now you see it! Now you don't!

THe ImPORTance OF RISK TaKING

Children need developmentally appropriate risk-taking experiences, such as climbing rope ladders and other structures, wrestling, scaling rocks, and splashing into puddles. They need to be able to go UP the slide and DOWN the steps and need not be restricted from sliding down on their tummy . . . in a train . . . with friends. They require freedom for jumping off swing sets, hanging from rope swings, swinging on their tummy, "spider swinging" (when two children face each other and swing together on the same swing), twisting themselves in swings, then letting go. And don't forget spinning so fast on the tire swing that every grown-up present feels the need to vomit, while the children are laughing with glee, learning about balance, motion, pendulums, cause and effect, action and reaction.

Risk taking encourages problem solving and critical thinking and has been identified as a fundamental prerequisite for fluent reading. In *Play's Place in Public Education for Young Children*, edited by Victoria Jean Dimidjian, we read that children who are afraid to risk rarely become fluent readers.

It is important that behaviors such as the ones I described above are allowed on playgrounds and that the enforcement of a large number of teacher-created rules are not taking the place of the facilitation of healthy, active, large-motor play. Take steps to ensure that any inside rules you have, like "no jumping," "no climbing," or "no running," do not follow the children when they head outside to play. I once visited a program right after a pretty big rainstorm. After nap, the teacher bundled up the children to go on a walk. "How exciting!" I thought. "A puddle walk!" Unfortunately what followed was the complete opposite. Not only did she spend the entire duration of the walk shushing all the children, she hollered at all of them for getting wet and jumping into puddles. I wanted to scream, "IF YOU DON'T WANT THEM TO JUMP IN THE PUDDLES, WHY DID YOU BRING THEM OUTSIDE?"

Sometimes when kids are outside, they want to just wander around, catch bugs, and play hand-clapping games. They welcome a break from lessons with a romp in fresh air. Other children, though, have more physical needs, and being outside is where they have the freedom to engage in them.

When I was a family child care provider, I would take the children on a walk or go to the park every day. Upon our arrival, some of the mothers at the park would grab their children, and dragging them across the parking lot to their cars, would sternly instruct, "Get in the van, get in the van now!" They said this because I was known to let children climb up the slide, as well as do other outrageously dangerous things like swing on their tummies, twist up in the swings, slide down the slide face first, and make wet sand for castles.

One woman in particular wouldn't pack up and leave the park but instead found it necessary to shake her finger at my children and constantly tell them, "NO!" "Don't!" "STOP!" and otherwise try to control the actions of everyone left at the playground.

One afternoon, my Dylan got on the swing and twisted it up all tight. He twisted and twisted and then he let go! He spun like crazy and became very dizzy. Of course, he did it again and again. On the third or fourth round of swing twisting, this woman approached Dylan, shook her finger and hollered, "That is not what you are supposed to do on the swings!" Dylan, almost falling over, reeling with the childhood delight of being dizzy, looked at her squarely and said, "Yeah, but I was doing physics." I had to hide behind the rock to conceal my laughter! She never again shook her finger at any of the kids.

Children need to move around. They cannot always sit still or use inside voices all the time. They do not have walking feet. Go outside as much as possible! Make time for active movement all day long. Run around, play tag, climb things, spin, jump, and remember that on those very, very hot days and very, very cold days you still can be moving! Don't think that you are exempt from MOVING just because it's too hot or too cold outside. Put on some music and dance. Learn, or relearn, some large-motor games that you can play both outside and in. Do the hokey pokey, play Ring Around the Rosie, dig down deep into your own childhood memory storehouse and remember what movement games you played when you were a child, then teach them to the children. Dust off that parachute, get some beanbags, and shake a leg!

I had a student one year who loved, and I mean *loved*, trains. I found a CD at the library that was nothing but instrumental train sounds with whistles and a rhythmic chugga-chugga choo-choo chorus. The children moved their arms back and forth, shuffled their feet, and would be trains all day long!

Another year I had a parent in our program who played the bagpipes. Occasionally he would pick his son up early and would bring his pipes. And when he did . . . oh boy! The children would go crazy with the dancing! Running, spinning, twirling, jumping all to the loud, but lovely, sounds of bagpipes.

We spend hours dancing, running, jumping, and hopping. We spin in circles and climb the rope ladder. We play tag, crawl on the grass, and swing on our tummies. We climb up the slide, shake the parachute, do the hokey pokey and dance to the "pa-pipes." If anyone walks in and asks what we are doing, I stand up strong and proud and tell them confidently that we are getting ready for kindergarten.

THE IMPORTANCE OF MOVING: A REVIEW

1. Children must move in order to learn.

2. Recess is being eliminated in the name of readiness and higher test scores.

3. The three main learning styles are visual, auditory, and kinesthetic. We use all three, but each person has preferences as to how to take in information.

4. Recess is not wasted time.

5. Inactivity often gives the false impression of hyperactivity.

SOME THINGS TO THINK ABOUT

1. Does my current program provide enough time for moving?

2. What is my own personal movement level? Am I an active person? Or more sedentary?

3. Do I make time for both *large-* and *small-*motor movement activities on a daily basis? What are some examples?

4. Might I need to modify this in some way to better meet the needs of the children in my class or program?

5. What are my personal thoughts on outside playtime and recess?

6. Where, how, and what did I play when I was a child?

7. What is my personal and professional understanding of ADHD?

8. Before reading this chapter, was I aware that telling a parent their child might have ADHD is *diagnosing* and out of the scope of my work?

9. Are there children in my class who might be unfairly labeled?

10. Are there ways for me to make the environment more interesting and engaging for these particular children?

11. Given there is a whole DAP domain set aside for *physical* development, how might I link making time each day for MOVING to the other domains: cognitive, language/literacy, and social/emotional development?

12. What steps can I take to be more confident when pointing out these developmental connections to parents? colleagues? naysayers?

13. What is one thing I can do Monday to begin making more time each day to move?

Notable and Quotable

Sitting still and being quiet is not a marketable job skill.

—Diane Trister Dodge, *The Creative Curriculum*

Movement is the door to learning.

—Paul E. Dennison, *Brain Gym*

We were conceived in motion, born in motion, and we must continue to move in order to learn!

—Mary Rivkin, *The Great Outdoors*

Gotta keep movin' to keep movin' my mind!

—Dr. Bill Michaelis, San Francisco State University

Attention deficit disorder does not reflect children's attention deficits but our lack of attention to their needs.

—Peter R. Breggin, M.D.

To "pin down" a thought, there must be movement.

—Carla Hannaford, *Smart Moves: Why Learning Is Not All in Your Head*

12

Make Time Each Day to . . . SING

I WAS FORTUNATE to attend many early childhood workshops presented by Tom Hunter before he died. Although his contributions were many, one thing that especially stands out was his advice about conference sessions. He used to say that when it comes to inappropriate, demeaning, fake, cheese-ball sessions, don't be afraid to RUN! If someone is talking about doing something with, or to, children that isn't appropriate, get your butt up out of the chair and RUN! He even suggested carrying signs that said RUN! So you could encourage others to do the same instead of being polite and nice and tolerating crap advice. But I digress. While he was an advocate for honesty, play, and being real with children, he was also a darn good musician. Once, at the beginning of a session he asked, "What songs do you know? Who taught them to you?" Hands shot up! People called out: "You Are My Sunshine," "Red River Valley," "When Johnny Comes Marching Home Again," "Tom Dooley," "My Bonnie Lies over the Ocean," "Oh! Susanna" and "She'll Be Coming around the Mountain."

What songs do *you* know? Who taught them to you?

Who are you teaching them to?

I learned songs from Miss Mary, from my parents, at camp and school, with Scouts, from church, and from my grandparents. My grandma sang and whistled through the house all day long. It was a family joke that no matter what phrase, comment, or question anyone ever stated around Grandma, she could sing a song that went with it. (And she could.) Show tunes were her specialty, and friendly (OK, fierce) competitions would emerge when we gathered together. Who could identify the most songs? Grandma always won. Our defeat inevitably led to a mad rush to the library (now we'd turn to Netflix!) to watch and listen to recordings of movie and stage musicals so we could "brush up" for next time.

We never quite achieved the Norman Rockwell experience of standing around a piano, with all the cousins and relatives belting out tunes while Grandpa played guitar and Grandma kept time on the piano, but we did sing while riding in the car and as we played around the house. We were exposed to a variety of music: the Beatles, Led Zeppelin, Herb Alpert, show tunes, and big band, and my dad had a not-so-secret infatuation with Iron Butterfly's infamous rock hit "In-A-Gadda-Da-Vida."

According to Howard Gardner, musical intelligence (one of eight kinds of intelligences he identified) is the first one we acquire and the last one we lose before we die. Musical intelligence begins while still in utero as the baby is exposed to the boom-boom-boom of the mother's heartbeat. Have you ever taken young children singing or caroling at a senior citizens' center? Many of our elderly parents and grandparents might not remember what they had for breakfast, the names of their children, or their phone numbers, yet they know all the words to "Amazing Grace."

Leading childhood expert Bev Bos refers to songs as "hooks to hang a memory on." If we know that it will be *songs* that stay with children their whole life, it seems to me that it is our responsibility to ensure they have something to remember. Over the years, workshop audience members have shared with me heart-wrenching stories of the power of music. The individual details are varied, but similarities run throughout—a family member is in a coma, hooked up to machines in a hospital, no recognition, no signs of being alert. Then someone comes in, inspired by a recently read article, and sings the songs they used to sing together. Instantly eyes open, hands are squeezed, there's a blip on the monitor . . . tears, goose bumps. An emotional feat that would be impossible if in fact songs had not been sung together and passed from one generation to the next.

Lullabies are so much more than quiet times and cuddles in the wee hours of the night. Singing songs lays the groundwork for listening skills and language development, yet we often find ourselves resisting because we have convinced ourselves that "we can't sing." Guess what? Those very young children can't sing either! I mean seriously, have you ever really listened to them? Therefore, I hereby give you permission to no longer worry about this! I mean it—really! It doesn't matter! Learn some songs and start singing them! Push through whatever hang-up you have about singing being the same as performing! This is where we get stuck. We go to a workshop, gather up some new songs, and then head back to the classroom on Monday. We say, "Come on over, kids! Let's sing a song!" You are ready! You knew all the words (yesterday)! You were confident (yesterday)! And now, as twenty sets of wide eyes stare at you from the circle-time carpet you FREEZE! Your throat gets tight . . . you get sweaty . . . you begin to panic . . . your heart is racing . . . you open your mouth to sing . . . *nothing!*

"Uh, maybe we'll put a CD on!" or "Um, wait guys. I think I recorded it . . . " (grabs smartphone).

Let them hear your voice. I was subbing once and was singing "You Are My Sunshine" not really to anyone in particular—just to the air. One little boy came up to me and said, "Hey you! My daddy sings me that whenever he wants me to try my best!" I don't know what that means, but yet I do not see it as my job to figure out what it means. I see it as my job to keep on singing.

I encourage you to dig into your memory storehouse! Start by singing the songs you remember, or start with the ones you and the children already know. The trick is to subtly start filling your day with a little bit more singing and remembering to resist the urge to make a performance out of it! We bog ourselves down with needing to sing it right, on pitch, and in key, and we riddle ourselves with performance anxiety. Don't turn it into a performance—start by singing to the air. How? Pick one song that you know, and start singing it when you are in the car, folding laundry, waiting in line at the store, when you hear a baby crying, preparing meals, giving the children a bath . . . no pressure, no performance, just a song—a song for you and a song for the children. The song will become a hook for your family to hang a memory on.

The belief of thinking we can't sing has only emerged in the last few decades, and it has coincided with the rising popularity of commercial, studio-enhanced recorded music. But when we leave singing to the professionals, we lose the power of our own voice. Infants and young children are not judging your voice by professional standards; instead they are focused on the eye contact, attention, and interaction they are receiving from you.

Children play with sounds by banging on drums, pots, and pans, shaking tambourines, and pounding the xylophone. I've seen many schools with "sound walls," which are simply fences hung with objects for the children to tap, bang, and otherwise "make music" on. Fill your environment with rhythm sticks, bells, drums, tambourines, pots and pans and wooden spoons, rain sticks, gourds filled with beans, and even film canisters filled with pebbles and sand for shaking.

When funds are available, we download and stream from the Internet. When they're not, we get used CDs from the library or the record store. The technology of music has changed drastically since I started teaching. I am sure many of you feel the same way! It seems as though in more recent times the *record player* is only hauled down off the top shelf whenever we are going to do spin art. But one day I wanted to play a song from a real vinyl album for the children to hear. I slowly pulled it out of the sleeve while the children watched with anticipation. As I took it out of the jacket and held it up carefully by the edges (weren't we all taught that?), Katie stood up and announced to the class, "We have those at home, but ours are small and shiny!"

In addition to suddenly feeling old, I realized, in one brief instant, that none of the children in front of me would have memories of saving money for 45s and LPs, no late-night slumber parties spent watching the album spin around and around, no lessons on learning how to be careful with the needle or the proper way of holding the album by its edges, and no frustrating moments of dealing with the "skips." Instead, a world of MP3 players, online streaming, music downloads, and iTunes will make up their childhood musical experience. Is this bad? Of course not. My only suggestion is for you to still learn the words and continue to sing WITH them. Don't let the professionals take your voice away!

Once I had the experience of shadowing a four-year-old who was attending a preschool near my home. He had no speech. The child had been through a whole gamut of tests, assessments, and ear exams, only to discover nothing. I do not necessarily jump to the conclusion that something is "wrong" when children do not speak. Sometimes, yes, there can be hearing issues, maybe a language delay. Sometimes it is a power struggle. Sometimes children just don't have anything to say to us yet. Sometimes they talk at school and not at home or vice versa. In this case the parents, teacher, and director called me in mostly as an extra set of eyes, ears, and hands, to see if someone in a more objective position could shed some insight. I agreed to come on-site twice a week to work with him.

To once again paraphrase Jane Healy: children need experiences to attach words to. So the first thing I did was offer a lot of time to explore mud, sand, and water. It is my experience that these raw materials serve as a great entry point into the realm of play, and often language development progresses from early experiences with these basic materials ("My shovel!" "Look at this!" "I want a bucket," etc.).

From here, we began to explore the yard and increase his level of physical activity. With the assumption that language springboards off the experiences a child has, we continued to look and search for his "backdoor." What did he need from this place that he was not receiving? So we played in the water, offered trucks, built with blocks, and squished with clay, all the while attaching loads of descriptive language to each interaction. We'd transition to something new after a turn on the swings with a song. He sat on my lap, and we would swing as I would sing, "My Bonnie lies over the ocean, my Bonnie lies over the sea." This was our ritual, swinging and singing, back and forth, "My Bonnie lies over the ocean."

It seemed our routine was a verbally descriptive play period punctuated by movement and singing. After some time, he started to say *water, mommy, daddy* and *cookie*, all in the proper context. But I was stubborn and wondered on my last day with him if I really had made an impact—really? Only four words? What might I have done differently? (Egos and a desire to overachieve can sometimes get in the way.)

When it was time to go, I gave him a hug and kiss, told him I would miss him, and went to my car. That night one of the teachers called me at home and said that as soon as I drove away, he went to the swings, hopped on, and while pumping in the way that only four-year-olds do, began singing, "My Bonnie lies over the ocean, my Bonnie lies over the sea."

Two weeks later he started talking. We found his backdoor, and it was music.

Making it Meaningful

Try to make sure that the music you select for children goes beyond being superficially entertaining. A lot of what is called "children's music" is a waste of time and money. It's trite, overly cute, sugary sweet, and lacks depth. Instead of "cute" children's music, try some jazz, some blues, a Bach concerto, folk songs, or a Sousa march! Real music and real songs are so much more significant and satisfying than educationally contrived songs about toothbrushing, traffic lights, or the days of the week, all which are sung to the tunes of either "Jingle Bells," "Row, Row, Row Your Boat," or "London Bridge." Seriously, do not be afraid to develop and *use* your "this is a load of crap" filter. Just because something is for sale in the children's section doesn't mean it's worth your money! It doesn't mean it's quality! Just because it's for sale in the vendor hall of an early childhood conference doesn't guarantee it is of quality either. If you think it's a stupid song, then it probably is. I don't care if the CD is only a dollar, you and the kids deserve better. There are a million unsung songs lying around waiting to be sung. They're ten times deeper and lots more meaningful than songs like these. Sing them.

Early in my career I was encouraged by leading educator, author, and recording artist Bev Bos to stop singing songs that *teach* and instead sing the songs that *include*. Up until learning this from her, I was guilty of singing the hundreds of silly, cutesy songs that all had the same tune. She encouraged me to sing to the air. She taught us songs that encouraged active participation from the children— songs that begged them to holler out words, phrases, and suggestions! Songs like "Uncle Jesse," where the children holler out what *they think* Uncle Jesse is wearing as he comes through the field; "Rainbow 'Round Me," where children say what *they see* outside of their window; and "The Pirate Song," where children say what *they did* on the day they jumped aboard the pirate ship. Learn songs that encourage active participation and involvement from the children, and sing them. Seize every opportunity to sing again and again with your children!

I taught in one school where the only singing that ever really went on was on Friday when the self-professed "Music Man" would come into the preschool, set up all his equipment, and then proceed to sing *at, to,* and *for* the children, never *with* them. He had shiny instruments and a keyboard that no one was allowed to touch. Children would holler out a song request (always while he was singing, of course), to which he'd respond, "Not right now. Right now we're singing about the days of the week. Come on! Join me! We all know the words!"

I just wanted to unplug his amp. I threatened a boycott. I wrote a letter to the administration. They told me I could be excused from the Music Man but that it was providing an enrichment experience for the children. A *what?*

Please don't save songs for assemblies and holidays. Sing them now. Sing them in the bathroom, in the shower, in the tub, in the rain, in the kitchen, and in the car! Sing them quiet, sing them loud, tap out patterns on your legs, on pots and pans, and on the steering wheel. Tap glass jars filled with varying levels of water, and listen to the different sounds and tones they make. Use wooden spoons to bang on the hubcaps you find on the side of the road. Chant. Find a Tibetan singing bowl, and play it. Sing because it allows you to express yourself, sing to convey ideas and express your moods. Sing for sheer enjoyment. Sing. Make music! And include the children.

Not sure of where to start? I have included a short list of "favorite songs" at the end of this section to get you off and running, but until then, do you like the Beatles? Put them on! Classical? Turn up the Mozart! Is country more your style? Bring it on! At my former family child care home, we played bagpipe music every afternoon. The neighbors must have loved it when the children screamed, "THE PA-PIPES! PLAY THE PA-PIPES!" But how could you NOT honor a request made by little ones who were so obviously moved by the experience? How could you turn it off? They would march around and pump their elbows (mimicking playing the pipes). Their eyes were so bright! You could almost see the music getting under their skin and moving their bodies. (I selfishly wonder sometimes, now as those children are older, if they remember those afternoons whenever they have the occasion to hear bagpipes play. Hooks to hang memories on.)

If you don't know the words, find someone who does, and ask them to teach you. Use what you have. Old-school tapes and CDs? Fine. YouTube? Excellent. Search for the words and download the music? Doesn't matter. Just learn the words. When I was a college student, one of our professors wouldn't pass you in her movement and music class until you got up in front of the room and taught your fellow students one hundred fingerplay songs. One hundred. Why? Because she was brilliant. She knew if she had you memorize only twenty, by the time you graduated, you'd have ten, and by the time you got your first job, you'd have two or three still rattling around up there. But that is a potential disaster! If all you've got is "I'm A Little Teapot," the kids will call you out by the third day of school for being a one-hit wonder! By "making us" learn more than a hundred, we had a good chance of still having more than a dozen by the time we were doing our first circle times. Do yourself a favor, memorize the classics, new favorites, and ones you steal, I mean *hear*, from the teacher down the hall. In the wise words of Sharron Krull, "Creative teachers are not born; they are made by the teacher next door."

Be sure to have music in the background during the school day; just don't get stuck there and forget the importance of singing around the carpet, singing under the tree, singing around a fire, and singing to the air. Prerecorded music, no matter the platform you use, should not be used as a substitute for singing together out loud.

I encourage you to go back and remember the songs and music of your childhood. What do you remember? Hand-clapping games? jump-rope songs? church songs? instruments? radios? those little 45s? the bulky 8-track tapes? It's time to tap into the power of music and provide it for the children. And it is not as hard as you might think! Sing in the shower, while doing dishes, while cleaning the house, while driving across country, or while walking to the market. Sing out loud, sing with the dog, sing with your family, and sing with the children. Grab that dusty old clarinet from seventh grade. Restring that old guitar. Teach children the songs, the words, and the melodies of their histories and their cultures.

If we know that music is the first intelligence acquired and the last one lost, it is our job to provide children with that which they will remember.

some songs to get you started

Alouette (If you love me, tell me that you love me)

Are You Sleeping? (Frère Jacques)

Did You Feed My Cow?

Go Tell Aunt Rhody

My Grandfather's Clock

Happy Birthday

I'm A Little Teapot

Go In and Out the Window

If You're Happy and You Know It

Mary Had a Little Lamb

The Muffin Man

My Bonnie Lies Over the Ocean

Oh! Susanna

Rainbow 'Round Me

Red River Valley

Skip to My Lou

This Old Man

Twinkle Twinkle Little Star

Uncle Jesse

Yankee Doodle

You Are My Sunshine

Favorite Children's Musicians

Ellen Allard

Bev Bos

Tom Chapin

Jim Gill

Greg and Steve

Hugh Hanley

Bill Harley

Tom Hunter

Dr. Jean

Ella Jenkins

Michael Leeman

Thomas Moore

Okee Dokee Brothers

Hap Palmer

Peter, Paul, and Mary

Raffi

Pete Seeger

Sharon, Lois, and Bram

Trout Fishing in America

Vincent Nunes

Dan Zane

THE IMPORTANCE OF SINGING: A REVIEW

1. Sing to the air! It doesn't need to be a performance.

2. You do not need to "know how to sing" to start singing.

3. Songs are "hooks to hang a memory on."

4. You will remember all the songs you learned from your childhood.

5. Musical intelligence is the first acquired and the last to go.

SOME THINGS TO THINK ABOUT

1. Are we singing enough?

2. Do my worries about the quality of my voice get in the way?

3. What songs do I know?

4. Who can I teach them to?

5. What was my childhood experience with music, singing, and songs?

6. How is music and singing influencing (whether positive or negative) the school environment?

7. Does my classroom provide enough opportunities for making music?

8. Music technology has changed drastically—how am I utilizing prerecorded music used in the classroom?

9. What song will I use to begin singing to the air?

10. Have I been guilty of singing everything to the tune of "London Bridge"?

11. Do any of our clients or families have musical talents or songs they'd be willing to bring in and share?

12. How are we meeting the child's cognitive, language/literacy, social/emotional, and physical developmental needs through musical and SINGING experiences provided each day?

13. What steps can I take to be more confident when pointing out these developmental connections to parents? colleagues? naysayers?

14. What is one thing I can do Monday to begin making more time each day to sing?

Notable and Quotable

Children's music often does nothing more than superficially entertain the young.

—Marvin Greenberg, *Your Children Need Music*

I've never found anything more powerful than sound and voice and music to begin to heal and transform every aspect of people's lives.

—Mitchell Gaynor, M.D., *The Sounds of Healing*

I would never sing a song with children that I wouldn't also sing with adults.

—Bev Bos

If singing were all that serious, frowning would make you sound better.

—Pete Seeger

Violence in our time stems from not teaching music to the young.

—Polybius, 2nd century BCE (attributed)

13

Make Time Each Day to . . . DISCUSS

TO LEARN LANGUAGE, children need to talk! Through talking and listening, we learn how to organize our thoughts, communicate, problem solve, and develop social skills. Children ask questions, tell elaborate stories, and ramble on incessantly! Many of us have experienced the frustration that comes with the twenty-fifth "Mommy, how . . . ?" "Daddy, what . . . ?" or "Teacher, why . . . ?"

Children continually want to talk about their ideas, experiences, new shoes, lunch box, belly buttons, and any other new discovery. Out loud! Carla Hannaford reminds us that it is not until around age seven that children develop what we might call "inner speech" or "self talk." Prior to this, children *literally* think out loud. This can sometimes cause trouble because well-meaning adults often think that everything a child says needs to be responded to. It doesn't. This is a tricky statement to make. Why? Because if it's taken out of context, it might appear as though I'm saying, "Don't talk with children," which is *not* what I'm saying. What I mean is not everything requires a response because not everything is for you!

This realization prompted me to blow the dust off some of psychologist Carl Rogers's books and revisit what is known as *reflective listening*. This is when you essentially repeat back what you hear someone say without commenting on it. You mirror their words back to them. The intention behind this is that the speaker will *hear* that you *heard* him, and if there is more to say, he will elaborate. The same is true with children. If you reflect their statements back to them, and they have more to add, this invites them to do so. It also invites them to say nothing in return. Which is also OK.

We aren't psychologists by any means, but this has really allowed me to have MUCH more meaningful conversations with children.

Let's examine another reason meaningful conversations can be tricky. Imagine you can have a bunch of kids on a carpet "reading" aloud to themselves or to each other and no one appears to be reading at all with all the talking and commenting going on. In her classic book *Smart Moves*, Carla Hannaford writes that the need to talk out loud and hear one's own voice is so great that some experts feel that silent independent reading is essentially ineffective until approximately age seven! In *The Child and the Machine*, authors Alison Armstrong and Charles Casement add that around this same age, children begin to learn how to internalize language (read: self talk) in order to figure out what they want to say before saying it out loud. This process allows them to "hear" what they want to say in their mind before actually saying it; this is called the "prelude to the ability to engage in rational thought."

Talking is essential to language development and thinking. When children have the opportunity to talk things through and verbally process new ideas, their thoughts become anchored in understanding. Nevertheless, a willingness to facilitate such verbal processing often decreases when a child enters school. Why? In a nutshell, it's too noisy! And even though we know children process information more effectively when they are allowed to move around and talk out loud, children working in groups, sharing ideas, and solving problems are often viewed as noisy, chaotic interruptions to the school day.

A stern command to "Sit down and be quiet!" is quite inappropriate. Why? Because it brings three major experiences young children need—moving around, touching stuff, and talking—to a screeching halt. What kind of learning is going on when everything is put away? When everyone is sitting still? When everything is quiet? Children need to be moving through their environment, manipulating materials, problem solving, and asking questions. These are impossible tasks when sitting still and keeping quiet is the real, albeit perhaps unspoken, objective.

Discussion Destroyers

I have compiled a list of what I call Discussion Destroyers. Discussion Destroyers prevent us from having engaging conversations, often without us realizing it. *I was guilty of doing all of them for a long time.* Please remember, though, that like so many other things, Discussion Destroyers are nothing more than habits. And with time and commitment, habits can be broken. Here's what I did:

* First, I became aware of behaviors I was engaged in.

* Second, I decided that I didn't want to do them anymore.

* Third, I was very patient with myself.

* Fourth, I recorded myself with the children so I could listen to how I spoke to/with them. (Save this for when you are further along in your journey.)

Oh boy! What an eye-opener! This fourth one here is what really helped me break the Discussion Destroyer habit! But please, hear me out on this! DO NOT, I repeat, DO NOT do it right out the gate unless you are really ready to start working! Please be advised that capturing a video or audio recording of yourself will TOTALLY jump-start your self-investigative process! We don't "do" Discussion Destroyers on purpose to be malicious; we do them because we don't know any better (or because we are on autopilot and not really *listening* to what we are saying). Until you realize there might be a different way of doing something, you're going to do it the way you know how. It takes TIME, patience, and commitment to change your mind. I feel I can be this direct in my writing because early on I noticed I was engaged in these behaviors, and I decided to change my mind. I give you permission to take the time to do the same.

DISCUSSION DESTROYER 1: ASKING A CHILD A QUESTION YOU ALREADY KNOW THE ANSWER TO

This is one of those tricky suggestions we hear from our mentors, yet still find ourselves guilty of doing. Bev Bos used to tell us this *all the time*. I knew on some level to not do it. Yet I still did it. I didn't really internalize the deeper lesson until one time I asked a child who was painting at the easel, "What colors are you using?" And I kid you not—he looked at me, looked at his painting, and then, to the air, for the benefit of any classmate in earshot, he boldly announced, "Hey guys! Ms. Lisa doesn't know her colors!" Here endeth the lesson.

When you see a child drip yellow and blue food coloring onto white shaving cream and then mix it up and make green, interrupting her experiment by asking, "What colors did you use?" is not engaging her in a discussion. It is a test to see if she knows her colors. It is searching to find what she "learned," instead of celebrating the process and discovery of making green.

A more appropriate response, if it was determined that one was actually necessary in the first place, might be, "Do you need anything else?" or "Look at that!" or possibly, "What else can I get for you?" Most of the time, though, I find that a supportive, encouraging *nonverbal gesture,* such as moving the can of shaving cream closer within reach, is all the adult interaction that's really necessary.

 DISCUSSION DESTROYER 2: DISREGARDING A CHILD'S ANSWER TO A QUESTION BECAUSE YOU WERE HUNTING FOR THE "RIGHT" ANSWER

I once watched a teacher sit in front of the calendar during group time and work her way around the circle asking each child, "What day is today?" In addition to being a question she already knew the answer to, she was on the prowl for the right answer to boot. Of course, being three, four, and five years old, *everyone* had a response, and *everyone* wanted a turn to share. Their answers ranged from "It's the weekend!" to "Yesterday!" to "It's my birthday" (it wasn't) to "Morning!" Of course none was "correct," but the teacher was waiting for the "right" answer. She spent ten minutes saying, "Nooo, noooo, nooo," "Not really," "OK, yes, but nooo," until, *finally*, Jenny said, "It's Friday!"

The teacher beamed at Jenny. Everyone else was silent. Then, as if on cue, it became apparent that *everyone* now had something to say about *Fridays*. There were comments about how Friday was "go-home" day, and they needed to bring their nap sheets home. There were cheerful announcements of how daddy visits on Friday. Someone said her family always gets pizza and a movie for Friday. Then someone announced that *next Friday* (of course) he was going to take a trip to grandpa's house to see the new puppy! This, of course, prompted a well-timed comment from Jeannie, who had just gotten a puppy for her *birthday*, which of course turned into a group inquiry of "How many days until *my* birthday?"

And right in the middle of this wonderful dialogue, the children were hushed and shushed because now it was time to sing the days-of-the-week song, which, of course, was to the tune of "Alouette."

Talking about it (whatever *it* may be) facilitates a child's ability to put thoughts into words. It encourages communication skills and assists the child in developing awareness of others outside of herself. This is a very important task when it comes to self-regulation and the development of executive functioning skills. Discussing *it* assists in language development, exposes children to new vocabulary, and encourages them to use their imagination as they create mental pictures to attach to someone else's story.

Schedules do not make time for these important happenings—people do.

 ## Discussion Destroyer 3: Any time you say, "someone already said that"

The next time you find yourself interacting with children in such a way that requires them to provide you with responses, such as voting or singing songs where they get to suggest some of the words, practice *not saying*, "Someone already said that."

Why? Young children are the center of their own universe, and as such they are often completely unaware of the other children around them. When you are singing "Here comes Uncle Jesse, he's runnin' through the field . . . with his horse and buggy and he knows just how you feel. He's hollerin' _____" (children fill in the blank here) and Mark shouts out that Uncle Jesse's hollerin' "RED PANTS!" you *know* that not two verses later someone else is going to shout out the same thing!

Although it's tempting to think these preschoolers are intentionally trying to get your goat, it's more probable that the second child didn't hear Mark say it first! And even if she did—so what! Sing it again! Resist the urge to say, "Someone already said red pants" WITH ALL YOUR MIGHT.

Discussion Destroyer 4: Asking Children Simple "Yes" or "No" Questions

Avoid yes/no (closed-ended) questions in favor of open-ended questions that promote thought and discussion. The invitation to "Tell me about your weekend" will solicit a more thoughtful response than "Did you have fun this weekend?" But *only if* you really care about the child's response *and* if you take the time to wait for it. It takes children time to respond to your queries. If you are asking questions, take the time to wait for the answers. Children, like adults, are pretty clever. I'm sure that at some time you've been asked a question and can tell that the person who asked didn't really care two bits about your response. Or you have met people who ask questions only to get the conversation to circle back to them and their interests. Intentional, thoughtful questions can spark lively debates, discussions, and conversations between children and children, adults and adults, and children and adults! Be willing to go beyond the easy yes/no formula. It takes a little more effort, but the conversations will be well worth it.

Discussion Destroyer 5: Asking "Fake" Questions

There are two kinds of fake questions. The first kind are those that appear to be choices but aren't really. Example: When I yell across the playground, "Are you guys ready to go in?" They say, "No!" But I ignore their answer and tell them to line up anyway. That's a fake question. Here's another fake question dialogue:

"Are you ready for bed?"

"No!"

"Lie down!"

Why did you ask if it wasn't really a choice? If it's time to go in, say, "It's time to go in." If there really isn't room for a back-and-forth banter, don't ask; otherwise it turns into an attempt to have a rational debate with a toddler—which is impossible. You will always lose. Why? Because eventually you just want the child to be quiet.

The other kind of fake question pops up when we forget how literal young children are. Example: When I say, "Can you go put this on the shelf?" and the three-year-old looks me in the face, says, "Yes," then walks away. Unlike adults, young children do not see my question as a polite request. They interpret it as an honest inquiry. Can you do this? Why, yes, I can!

Discussing Leads to Problem Solving

Contrary to popular belief, children do not talk all day to drive us crazy. They are processing their observations and their experiences. By encouraging and facilitating discussions, we help children to understand their world and how it works. This is one reason why it is important to use *descriptive language* when speaking with children. Enthusiastically pointing out the "*beautiful red cardinal* that is *perched* on the *wooden* fence" provides so much more than "Look at the bird."

When we adults talk through our day and think out loud, we are showing children how to identify a problem, consider a solution, make a plan, and take action. We're also modeling impulse control and the power of reflecting on a situation instead of just reacting. Here are a couple of examples:

* ✿ "We're all out of chicken, so I think I'm going to cook macaroni for lunch today."

* ✿ "Oh shoot, we are all out of yellow paint. I didn't notice that yesterday. Which color would you like instead?"

I call this "putting yourself on speakerphone." I have found it beneficial for everyone, not just the children. It encourages me to be patient and thoughtful as well as mindful of my actions. It also encourages me to stay in the present moment, which is very important when working with children. By watching and hearing me think out loud, the children are able to observe the problem-solving process in action. I am modeling the skills I want them to develop. By including them in the process, you are increasing communication and socialization skills.

Learning how to communicate with others is a skill that remains long after cubby tags have faded and the preschool art has disintegrated in the boxes in the attic. Young children can easily acquire the skills needed for effective problem solving when the adults in their world are *consistent, patient,* and *committed* and when, of course, adults use good communication skills themselves! Children will do what we do. I was told once, "If you want them to do it, do it. If you don't want them to do it, don't do it." Actions *do* speak louder than words. We cannot develop effective problem-solving skills in children if we cannot do it ourselves.

We must take ownership of the process of teaching problem-solving skills. We cannot toss children back into playground battles over shovels with flip comments like "Go use your words." What "words" do you want them to use? Some children don't *have* words to use, and some children have words you don't want them to use! Like

So what is the secret for avoiding Discussion Destroyers? First of all, don't overthink it. There isn't a book to read or webinar to watch. It's good old-fashioned TIME. Taking the time, seriously, to think about what is about to come out of your mouth. Is it clear? consistent? direct? open-ended? Are you patient? Are you hurried? What is the intention behind the questions? Do you have TIME to wait for the response? I know, I know . . . you're busy . . . you have to do circle . . . you have to do snack . . . you have to change diapers—I get it! But I will remind you again that there is NOTHING more important than the relationships you are cultivating in your homes and classrooms. Relationships grow out of relevant, meaningful conversations. Snack can wait.

you, I know some of the "words" children know, and, also like you, I have witnessed Karen demanding her @%$*& shovel back! Just as Cassie announces, "&*%$ it! That's mine!" If you have not taken the time to teach and model what you want them to say, "Go use your words" is taking the easy way out and will not be effective.

The same is true with "I don't like it!" and "Stop it!" When I hear these phrases on the playground, I go up to the child saying them and ask, "What do you want her to stop doing?" or I'll ask, "What don't you like?" Then we proceed from there. I cannot stress the importance of being *specific* when talking with young children. Have you taught them effective language? Have you modeled the problem-solving techniques? Unless children have been coached on what tools to use, they will grab the ones closest at hand. They will use the ones that are the most comfortable and familiar but not necessarily the most effective.

Children can be taught how to make requests of each other. A simple "I want a turn on the bike when you're done" is how bikes are traded and turns monitored. An important piece to this negotiation is to ask the child who has announced a desire to have something, "What are you going to do while you are waiting?" Teachers should not get in the middle, count laps, mandate sharing, set timers, or in any other way interfere with the process of Colin figuring out how to ask Hannah for a turn on the bike when she's done. This takes time and a trust in the process. Eventually kids realize they get to have/use whatever the something is (bike, doll, truck, book) until they are *done*. When he is done, someone else might want it. And, in turn, once the second kid gets it, she knows that *she* gets it until *she* is done. After a couple weeks, no one is hoarding anything out of a fear that they will never get to use it again. And although you won't believe me until you see it, once children know this to be true, they will relinquish things because they are actually done. And they no longer need to hold on to something to fulfill some need for power and control.

Some of you are fortunate to have had many of the children in your program since they were infants; this means they've grown up in an environment that models this behavior. *When older children join your program, it is of utmost importance that they are modeled the same skills as the other children.* Some of them will have had a previous preschool experience, some will not. We must not assume that these children come to us with an understanding of problem solving simply because they are older.

Children do not learn how to get a turn on the bike after one "lesson" or a one-time modeling of how to do it. Modeling this skill requires the adults to be patient and consistent. Older children who have not yet been taught problem-solving skills can learn them. Grown-ups can learn them too; it just takes a little longer. The good news is that it's never too late.

The same modeling process holds true for teaching children how to speak out when they feel they have been harmed or wronged. "So-and-So took Such-and-Such's shovel," "I had it first," "He took it!" "It's mine!" Typical preschool politics. First and foremost, we do not allow children to be victims. If someone gets hit on the playground or in the classroom, the first thing we do is encourage the child who got hit to holler something like, "Don't hit me!" We teach children over and over again how to use a BIG VOICE when saying "no!" not a little whiny one. We encourage them to find the power in themselves and in their voice as they learn how to solve their problems. We do not pay a lot of attention to the child who did the hitting. This removes the power from the act of hitting and also deflates the possibility of receiving negative attention, which·some children crave.

Along with hitting and toy taking, tattling is another natural by-product of having a large number of children interacting with each other over any amount of time. Again, it is not fair to toss the child back into the drama with a simple "Nancy, go tell Sophie you want your doll back" when in fact Nancy might have never learned how to effectively do so. We must not skirt our responsibility of teaching children the words they need to get their dolls back.

Children know from both verbal and nonverbal cues that the teacher is there to help when needed. The teacher will walk back over to the other child with them and even assist in the coaching of the dialogue. Teachers are engaged, involved, modeling, and assisting as children learn how to solve their problems. Our ultimate goal is for the children to be able to communicate successfully with others independently, without needing to constantly rely on the grown-up to assist them.

There are also times along the way when you just need to back off and trust that the children can begin to handle things for themselves. When there is no immediate danger, it is sometimes best to let children play alone without a lot of hovering grown-ups. Some children spend *ten hours a day* together every single day of the week. I have learned that if I were to get involved with every single minor incident every hour of every minute of every day *I would go nuts*. Imagine if your mom got involved *every single time* you and your siblings or cousins or the neighbor kids had a conflict! You would never have had the chance to practice what she had taught you.

Teachers and parents are constantly providing skills and modeling appropriate behaviors. Sometimes it is necessary to stand close by and determine if we are teaching the right skills or behaviors. We are entrusted with teaching a skill that will have a lifelong impact. It is important to occasionally step back and assess our progress. Anna Quindlen stated, "Each day we move a little closer to the sidelines of their lives, which is where we belong, if we do our job right."

But What Are They Learning?

When preschool programs toss the importance of social and emotional skill development out the window in exchange for more rigorous, academic, technological, preparatory skill development, they are depriving children of skills necessary for their future social and academic success. Additionally, as I mentioned earlier in this book, when we focus on one part of development at the expense of another, we are *not* being developmentally appropriate. Remember the four domains of DAP? Social/emotional, physical, language/literacy, and cognitive. High-quality programs focus on all four. They don't skip over one, thinking that by pushing one aside it makes room for "more" of another. That's not how it works.

In *Set for Success: Building a Strong Foundation for School Readiness Based on the Social-Emotional Development of Young Children*, an in-depth report published by the Ewing Marion Kauffman Foundation, researchers summarized how social and emotional competence sets the foundation for school readiness. In the report they state:

> Research evidence from the National Academy of Sciences and others has demonstrated that children entering school with well-developed cognitive and social skills are most likely to succeed and least likely to need costly intervention services later through either special education or juvenile justice. The science of early childhood has repeatedly provided evidence that strong social-emotional development underlies all later growth and development. (1)

The report reminds us that that social/emotional development and academic achievement are not separate goals. Instead, echoing the tenets of DAP, the authors maintain that all of the developmental domains work together to strengthen a child's chance of school success. The report stresses that social and emotional well-being must be a priority if our goal is to have children entering school ready to learn and succeed.

It's not that social and emotional skills are more important than cognitive skills, it's just they've been ignored for so long that they often require an intentional "boost," as it were, because for too long now they have been shoved to the back burner in the name of "readiness." Because school readiness is intimately tied with social and emotional development, being ready to learn requires much more than knowing your ABCs and numbers.

But let's be honest. The real struggle is not with *our* understanding of this but rather in getting the *general public* to buy in. Everyone reading this book knows a young child who can identify the letters of the alphabet, play the violin, dance for grandpa, name geometrical shapes, recite her address, and count to one hundred in six different languages. *However*, when someone takes her shovel on the playground, she falls apart into a blubbering mess. Meltdown! Whining and crying, she runs to the teacher, wailing about her missing shovel, hollering and carrying on. Yes! She knows her name. Yes! She knows her colors. Yes! She knows her shapes. But guess what? *She doesn't know how to get her shovel back.*

And *children* who do not learn how to problem solve, discuss conflict, and communicate with others turn into *grown-ups* who can't do it either. Whiny lamentations over swiped toys, missed turns, and who is looking at whom will someday turn into even more annoying tirades about stolen parking spots, lost staplers, missing files, unfair deadlines, and selfish coworkers. It's no surprise that most adults who get fired from their jobs do not get fired because they can't do their work, but rather because they lack social and communication skills and never learned how to get their shovels, I mean staplers, back.

Compare this to an early childhood environment. Children *do not* get kicked out of child care centers for not knowing the ABCs or numbers. Are they given the boot if they can't tie their shoes or recite their phone number? Of course not! But many are asked to leave the program if they are constantly hitting, biting, kicking, and scratching—all of which indicate an absence of problem-solving capabilities and a lack of social skills.

When social and emotional competence is sacrificed in the name of knowing the ABCs, no one is really getting ready for anything. Who cares if she can count to one hundred if she is scared to get off the bus? Does it really matter if he can identify all the colors if he doesn't feel comfortable asking for clarification of the assignment the teacher just gave? What good is knowing how to write your name before you go to kindergarten if you don't know how to zip your coat or tie your shoes? Or wipe your butt?

The *Set for Success* report that I quoted previously tells us that children who lack social and emotional competence when they begin kindergarten are often plagued by behavioral, emotional, academic, and social development problems that follow them into adulthood. A follow-up article by Ronald Kotulak summarized the report by saying parents can increase a child's chance of success in kindergarten by fostering confidence, curiosity, motivation, cooperation, and *the ability to communicate* (emphasis added).

In their book *The Creative Spirit*, Goleman, Kaufman, and Ray suggest that hothouse training regimes that force math, reading, and writing before children have any real interest in doing these things are not only inappropriate, but often lead to an aversion of and to the subject being taught. In a fantastic keynote address, I heard Alfie Kohn remind teachers that "when something is forced down our throats, it has nowhere to go but back up."

When I was still doing family child care, I received a phone call from a woman who had heard about our program. She was looking for a preschool for her daughter and asked me to describe what we offer. I jumped into my energetic description of our play-based, hands-on, and hands-in, child-centered environment and was just about to tell her of the activities taking place that particular day when she stopped me with a heavy sigh. "Ohhhh," she said, "you're one of those *social-emotional* preschools." "Umm . . . yes," I said. She proceeded to inform me that her *neighbors* told her that if she put her daughter in a social-emotional preschool, she would never be ready for kindergarten. HER NEIGHBORS?

I gently told her that, in actuality, a social-emotional preschool is really the only kind of program that prepares children for kindergarten. I shared with her that we have piles of research that confirm the fact that the only children who benefit (long term) from an early preschool experience are children who have been in child-centered, play-based, social-emotional programs. I was on a roll, the soapbox had been placed on the floor, and I was proudly taking my place upon it! "Come see us!" I encouraged (or was it begged?). "Come observe! Watch what we do, and let your child have a go at it! What we are doing *is* kindergarten readiness. It just looks a little different than what your *neighbors* have in mind. Sometimes it's best to see it in action before making a decision!"

She stopped me midsentence and informed me that she just couldn't "take the risk of [her] daughter not being ready." Then she hung up. I stepped off my box discouraged, mad, angry, sad, and frustrated. I wanted to kick it across the room!

JUST BECAUSE THEY CAN
DOESN'T MEAN THEY SHOULD

I know we all want what is best for our children. Yet often what is being sold to you as best is not. I met a man who teaches toddlers how to read. He sees it as providing a service. I see it more as a trap. A trap that catches well-meaning parents and makes them think that by *not* teaching their babies how to read they are somehow providing a disservice for their children. In actuality, it is the complete opposite.

Beware of anyone who says anything to you like: "Oh, if your child doesn't read/write/know the alphabet/know numbers [choose one] by the time he is two/three/four/five [choose one], he will never succeed!" Or "College choices hinge on their performance in preschool!" I saw a poster once in an airport that said, "You might not be thinking about college, but we are." It was an advertisement for a child care center!

If you look deep enough, folks who say this kind of stuff are ultimately selling something. They prey on your emotions to coerce you to purchase their product. They do NOT have a vested interest in either you or your child. They want your credit card number. But because of our desire to provide for our children and do what we think is "best" (or what we are being sold as best), we become easy suckers to their medicine show and buy the "Do it quick! Do it NOW! Do it bigger! better! faster!" kit they are selling out of their carpetbag.

We think we are doing what is best. Everyone else is buying it. The neighbor kids all have one. The five o'clock news said it is what the best and brightest are using to "get ready." You have questions, but the medicine show has left. And so has your money. You look at the stuff left in exchange for your cash, and you can't help but wonder, "Will it help? Will it work?"

Meanwhile, our young ones are standing by twisting and pulling their hair. Their nails are gnawed down to the nubs. They are stressed. They have headaches, bellyaches, and constipation. BUT they can count to one hundred in three languages, spell their names, and know their shapes and colors. It calls to mind the fairy tale "The Emperor's New Clothes." Everyone drank the Kool-Aid. No one wanted to take responsibility and call the sneaky tailors to the carpet for pulling the wool over the emperor's eyes. It took a little boy, a *child*, to break the spell that, duh, everyone knew they were under, when he announced, "Yo! The dude's nude!" The honest words of a child finally broke the spell, which prompted hasty confessions of "Yes, well, I knew he was naked, but I didn't have the guts to admit it." I do not think it is too much of a stretch to say that when children "refuse" to come to circle, and engage in other acts of "defiance," they are in their own way telling us, "Yo! The Dude's Nude!"

What will it take for us to finally stand up and say, "Yo! You're right!" Just how far are we willing to go to secure our children's place in the dog and pony show? What are we sacrificing? When will it stop?

Do we want what's best for them? Of course we do. But the emperor's been naked for a loooong time, and it's about damn near time we point it out.

MUCH MORE THAN A CATCHY PHRASE!

Have you heard any of these chants that suggest changes in early childhood education?

- ✿ Down with dittos!
- ✿ Sooner is not better!
- ✿ Childhood is a journey, not a race!
- ✿ Education is not the filling of a bucket—it is the lighting of a fire!
- ✿ Too much, too fast, too soon is not the answer!
- ✿ Children learn through play!
- ✿ Preschool is not boot camp for kindergarten!

Battle cries such as these take the form of bumper stickers, T-shirts, buttons, and hashtags that we plaster all over our cars, bodies, backpacks, and social media posts. But slogans and hashtags aren't enough.

Please allow me to circle back to the Binder Challenge I mentioned in the introduction (page 2). You DID read that part, right? No? #SMH Well then, GO! Do it right now . . . I'll wait.

Are we good? Awesome!

As teachers, providers, and educators, we have a professional responsibility and, I would argue, an *obligation* to develop the ability to discuss and communicate our understanding of the research and the knowledge that supports playful learning.

We are then able to support that while "playing" with water, cotton balls, and eyedroppers, children are learning about absorption. When jumping off rocks, they are learning about gravity. When mixing cornstarch and water, they experience a suspension and create a non-Newtonian fluid. When blowing bubbles, they are exposed to the concept of surface tension. While "just scribbling" and painting on huge sheets of paper, they are mastering spatial representation. And when they dump vinegar onto baking soda, they are learning about action, reaction, and the properties of carbon dioxide.

There's more to creating a high-quality program than having the right equipment and an informational brochure that says you believe in developmentally appropriate practice. Educators must be able to call upon the research that supports their classroom practice—especially that which supports playful learning. When we are able to use research as well as anecdotal evidence when discussing our methods, we appear professional, confident, and credible. What more could a parent ask for?

THE IMPORTANCE OF DISCUSSING: A REVIEW

1. Be aware of the Discussion Destroyers.

2. Discussing = problem solving = learning how to get your shovel back.

3. The development of *all four* domains within DAP is a priority in all high-quality programs.

4. One domain is not highlighted at the expense of another, yet it is acknowledged that in recent years, social/emotional development has been ignored in the name of readiness. Because of this, some children might need an intentional intervention.

5. Do not be swayed by product pushers who are selling you something and really aren't vested in the true success of your child(ren).

6. Teaching problem solving takes commitment, time, and patience on the part of all grown-ups involved.

7. Educators have the responsibility to be able to discuss and articulate the "learning" that can be linked with the play-based experiences being provided for the children.

8. Have you accepted the Binder Challenge?

 # SOME THINGS TO THINK ABOUT

1. How does my program make time for open-ended discussions?

2. Do I struggle with problem-solving skills in my own life?

3. How do I currently assist my children in problem solving?

4. What might I need to do differently?

5. What is my comfort level with allowing children to figure things out for themselves?

6. Do I currently send them off unprepared to "use their words"?

7. What is my level of "descriptive word" usage?

8. Do I find myself often trapped by Discussion Destroyers?

9. Which one(s)?

10. Up until now did I see the links between discussing, social skills, and school success?

11. How can this information benefit my program and the children I serve?

12. Does some of this information need to be passed on to the parents and teachers in my program? When can I make that happen?

13. I know that communicating and problem solving clearly link to a child's social and emotional development. Can I explain how DISCUSSING also connects with the cognitive, language/literacy, and physical development domains?

14. What steps can I take to be more confident when pointing out these developmental connections to parents, colleagues, and naysayers?

15. What is one thing I can do Monday to begin making more time each day to discuss?

🦉 Notable and Quotable

If you want to have intelligent conversations with children, give your own assumptions a rest, put on your listening ears and hear what the child is really saying.

—Jane Healy, *How to Have Intelligent and Creative Conversations with Your Kids*

Parents can improve a child's chances of success in kindergarten by fostering a strong relationship that enhances confidence, independence, curiosity, motivation, persistence, self-control, cooperation, empathy and the ability to communicate.

—Ronald Kotulak, *Chicago Tribune*, September 6, 2000

*The more you practice listening to children, the more skilled you
will become. The most important thing is to remember that you are
listening for children's unique thinking about the world, not for them
to regurgitate facts to you.*

—Lisa Burman, *Are You Listening?*

Teaching children how to talk means teaching children how to think.

—Jane Healy, *How to Have Intelligent and Creative Conversations
with Your Kids*

*Take time to be in the moment with children and to give them the
time to form, create, and share ideas with you.*

—Lisa Burman, *Are You Listening?*

14

Make Time Each Day to . . . OBSERVE

AS GROWN-UPS WE put a lot of faith into what we can see, often forgetting we have four other senses, four additional ways of taking in information. When working with children, it is to everyone's advantage to provide opportunities that use all five senses.

Observing and discussing often go hand in hand as adults employ the use of descriptive language to assist children in noticing subtleties and nuances within their environment. What do you see? What is that smell? Do you hear that? Touch this! Mmmmm, this tastes good!

My Five Senses is a popular theme in many preschools because there are five senses and *five* days of the week. How easy it is to create lesson plans that explore one sense each day. There is nothing inherently wrong with smelling jars filled with cinnamon and cotton balls drenched in vanilla, playing Listening Lotto during circle time, reaching into mystery touch boxes, and having tasting parties filled with exotic fruits and different blends of juices. And don't forget experiencing what it's like to paint while blindfolded! But over the years while learning more about teaching (and changing my mind about how I did it), I grew to realize that saving the senses for one brief week of exploration simply wasn't enough time!

I learned that when we start paying attention to the sights and sounds around us, we increase the various ways we take in information. This leads to experiencing more of the wonder around us. There are many things in our world that we can see, look at, notice, and recognize, but when was the last time you really *observed* what surrounds you? When was the last time you *listened* to the sounds coming from the neighborhood or the playground? *Felt* the textures of the pillows in the book area or the clothes in home living? *Smelled* the scents emerging from a kitchen where applesauce is simmering and cookies are baking? *Watched* the ice block of colors melt in the afternoon sun? *Tasted* the salt on the made-from-scratch pretzels you whipped up with the children for snack?

Once again, not having enough time often becomes the roadblock to appreciating what our senses have to offer. We *need to believe* that hummingbirds sipping their sweet red nectar and mourning doves cooing in the trees are things worth paying attention to. If grown-ups feel that watching butterflies, listening to birds, and feeling the grass under our bare feet are silly wastes of time, no appreciation will transpire.

There must be enough time for exploring how the ooblick feels as it drips down our hands, arms, and legs. There must also be an understanding that some children can spend twenty, thirty, even forty minutes exploring the texture and feel of this goopy substance of cornstarch and water. There needs to be time carved out of the day for baking, cooking, and enjoying the smells that then permeate the room. This includes the awareness that the *process* of smelling spices, touching ingredients, and kneading dough is often more exciting and more important to children than the *product* that will emerge from the oven.

If the exploration is hurried, the experience will be lost. When we slow down enough to make and appreciate these discoveries, we unlock the door to a wider world for both ourselves and the children. Let's take a look.

THE SENSE OF TOUCH

We use our hands to take in information via our sense of touch. To experience touch and increase the children's "touch repertoire," teachers fill sensory tubs with such materials as sandpaper, cooked spaghetti, pudding for painting, cornstarch, clean mud (a mixture of warm water, grated bar soap, and toilet paper), cornmeal, sandbox sand, beach sand (there is a difference), birdseed, flaxseed (sometimes dry, sometimes with warm water, which creates a pleasing, squishy sensorial experience that calls up images of warm molasses), mud, dirt, beans, shaving cream, gelatin, rice, pebbles, rocks, ice, seashells, flour, and, sometimes, just plain old water.

We offer words such as *touch*, *feel*, *sticky*, *wet*, *dry*, *rough*, *bumpy*, *smooth*, *slick*, and *scratchy* as they describe the different ways we experience tactile sensations, the way we feel things. This is the attachment of language to experiences. We extend activities by offering scoops, funnels, and measuring cups. Forgotten and unused kitchen equipment, such as muffin tins, pie tins, wooden spoons, pots, and pans, find new lives in the hands of little children. We offer magnifying glasses to make the birdseed bigger, and safety goggles because then the children *know* they are really "working."

For children who don't want to touch with fingers and hands, we offer long sticks and wooden spoons so they can still have the experience without having to actually touch. All are invited to participate at their own level of comfort. We take sensory walks because although some children don't like to touch with their hands, they don't mind using their feet. So we put the sensory tubs on the floor and *walk through* the dirt, water, sand, or birdseed. We make "touch bags" filled with shaving cream, hair gel, corn syrup, sand, or gelatin, then zip the bags closed. Touch bags offer another way of experiencing textures for children who might not yet be comfortable thrusting their whole hand in a tub of clean mud. Not everyone needs or likes that high level of sensorial stimulation—some do and some don't. Make room for all comfort levels, and avoid forcing anyone to touch.

If you yourself do not like touching various textures, that's OK, but you need to be cautious about not transferring your hesitation to the children. I tell teachers, "I don't need you to like it, but I need you to make room for it." And be mindful of your facial expressions and body language. If you are squishing up your face while inviting children to "come touch," they are reading your face, not your words! No one is going to want to explore it if your body language is screaming *yuck!*

I also keep plastic gloves in the room. The children see me wearing them sometimes, and then, of course, they all want to wear them. Mikey especially loved the gloves. He wore them to play in the mud but also to ride the bike and bounce the ball. He wore them all over the school—inside! outside! "Sa-see! Sa-see!" he cried. (He never quite got "Lee-sa" as my name. To Mikey, I was "Sa-see.") "Take a picture with my gloves!"

Mikey put water in the gloves and then carried his "handbag" all over the place. He put on the high heels and the feather boa and wore his gloves around the house. I know when I wear gloves, things feel different, so we keep heavy-duty dish gloves, mittens, winter gloves, and clear disposable gloves for the children to experience different touch and textures too. Once while I was in the kitchen washing the dishes, Mikey came into the room. I heard him before I saw him as he *always* had on the gaudy gold bridesmaid shoes from the dress-up corner. He came around the corner where I was washing dishes, green heavy-duty plastic gloves up to my elbows. He actually shuddered in delight, eyes wide with longing, and said, "Nice gloves, Sa-see."

He wore them the rest of the day.

Some children seem to really enjoy (almost crave) tactile stimulation! Have you ever worn a pair of nylons around these children? They love the texture of nylons and really enjoy rubbing, pulling, and touching them. They really respond to the feel of the nylons under their little hands. Fill the environment with pillows that are made of different kinds of materials, such as satin, velour, corduroy, or anything else that provides an interesting texture.

Another fun project for touch exploration is to put a long sheet of contact paper on the floor, sticky side up! Peel off the backing, lay the contact paper down on the floor, and tape it down with the sticky side up. The children really enjoy putting hands and bare feet on it! They dance on it, walk on it, tiptoe on it, or sometimes just touch it with a finger or two.

You can tape bubble wrap on the floor or on a table for more tactile exploration! I keep pieces of sandpaper in the environment too. I find neat things to touch and bring them into the space to provide them for the children, always remembering to stay sensitive to varying comfort levels of touch.

While enhancing our environment with *things* to touch, we must never forget the power of *human touch*. Hugging, holding hands, wrestles and romps on the lawn, sitting on laps, back rubs before naptime, quick squeezes of support, and long sustained embraces of comfort all need to be a part of our daily experience with children too. Touching decreases stress. If your program discourages adults from touching the children enrolled in the program, you need to have a conversation about where that expectation came from. How is it possible to take care of children, model empathy, and deepen relationships when we are not permitted to touch one another?

I was told once that the school didn't want to "take any chances." I asked why they were hiring people they felt they might be "taking chances" with. And while *trust* is a topic worthy of its own in-depth investigation, for the time being let it suffice to say that if there is no trust, there are no relationships. And if there are no relationships, there is no program.

In her book *A Natural History of the Senses*, Diane Ackerman tells us that touch clarifies the shorthand of our eyes and reminds us that we live in a three-dimensional world. Run outside and soak it up! Plunge into an icy pool of water, feel the long grass tickle your ankles, or dive into that tub of ooblick. Put your arms in a bowl of Jell-O, put your bare foot in a mud puddle, and feel the tension of the earth and water as you try to pull it out. Feel the squish of wet sand between your toes, get a back scratch, a massage, or a head rub. You are on your way to understanding the importance of touch.

THe sense oF smeLL

When we try to explain or describe a smell, we often find ourselves at a loss for words. The sense of smell is often called the "mute sense" because it is the one with no words. Ackerman says we describe smells through metaphor—what they smell like in terms of other things (smoky, fruity, sweet), or we describe them by how they make us feel, (intoxicating, pleasurable, disgusting, revolting). The link between the language and smell center of our brain is very weak, thus our struggle with using words to describe smells, according to Ackerman.

The connection between the smell and memory centers, however, is very strong. Our sense of smell serves as our strongest link to memory. Smells become a virtual trip wire to our memory center, bringing back memories, recollections, and associations triggered by that smell. What smells trigger memories for you? Open a box of crayons and inhale deeply. What do you remember? What pictures come to your mind? How about a jar of paste? Ever walked into a crowded room and caught the scent of a former boyfriend? a past teacher? a family member?

A workshop participant recently shared that tea with lemon evokes memories of her grandmother. The smell of toasted rye bread and coffee in the percolator brings up memories of breakfast at my grandma's house. How about you?

Some programs ask that the infant's mother sleep in the same shirt for a few days before baby starts in the program. Then the teacher can wear the shirt draped over her own clothes so that the newborn can be connected with mom's familiar smell while making the transition to a new provider. The same idea worked for a baby once who was refusing to take a bottle. The little one just could not relax. She cried, arched her little body, and seemed inconsolable. I called her mom and asked her to sleep in a T-shirt for a couple nights in a row and then bring us the shirt. We draped the mom-scented shirt over our body, allowing the baby to "smell" mommy while taking her bottle. Success! Eventually she no longer needed the shirt while eating, but it was a big help during that rough transition.

One of my brothers has been a teacher in both Huntington Beach and Sacramento, California. One Monday morning one of his students came running into the classroom announcing, "Mr. Griffen! Mr. Griffen! I was at the mall this weekend, and I *smelled* you! I looked everywhere for you but but but . . . I couldn't *find you!*" Someone who was wearing the same cologne as my brother had walked by during her trip to the mall! She was *sure* that her Mr. Griffen was somewhere, and she couldn't understand why she wasn't able to find him! After all, she could *smell* him . . . where did he go? Can you just see her searching the mall, "Mr. Griffen? Where are you? Mr. Griffen?"

What perfume counter will *your* students walk by in five, ten, twenty years that will cause them to stop for a moment while they watch the video of memories playing in their mind's eye of the days they spent with you?

Many of the schools I visit lack "good" smells and instead only provide the smell of various cleaning fluids, like Pine-Sol, bleach, and Simple Green. These are not "cozy and warm" smells. They make me think of cold, sterile hospitals and oversanitized waiting rooms. Now don't get me wrong; you still need to *clean*. But by all means if the first thing you smell when you walk in the door every morning is bleach, *do something about it!* Make a pot of coffee every morning even if no one drinks it! It smells good. It's warm and inviting. Make scent jars for the environment (baby food jars with spices and extracts), plant fragrant herbs and plants, like rosemary, basil, heather, or lavender, and plunge your face in the roses. Bake bread, make pasta sauce, cookies, and pies. Try putting vanilla on the light bulbs. Burn candles, and light incense too.

I want the children to grow up and remember me, and their time with me, when they smell chocolate chip cookies, spaghetti sauce, rosemary, patchouli oil, and roses—not when they are walking down the janitorial aisle of the grocery store. "Ah, Simple Green! Smells like Ms. Lisa's house!" No no no!

I imagine you would want the same.

THe sense oF Taste

One year, much to everyone's surprise, while boiling a purple cabbage to obtain the purple juice for a science-related "acid and base" experience, four-year-old MacKenzie pointed to the cabbage simmering in the skillet and announced, "I want to eat some of that!" I went to the kitchen and got her a bowl, spoon, and fork and gave her some cabbage. I really didn't think she'd like it, but I wasn't about to tell her she couldn't try it! MacKenzie sat down with that bowl of cabbage and ate it up quickly and with great pleasure. She asked for seconds even before we realized she had started eating the first serving. Then, of course, the entire class demanded some! Science turned into snack that day!

Cook together, eat together, and take your time while eating. Chew your food, and savor the flavors. When I was running a program, I encouraged parents to pack lunches filled with food from the previous night's dinner, or a sandwich, a fruit, or veggie and maybe a cookie or two. I discouraged fast, easy, convenience-style foods and prohibited candy and soda. No one is forced to eat, and the children can eat their food in any order they like. Lunch is a time for conversation, relaxation, the discussion of the morning's events, as well as the preparation for the transition to nap and rest time. It's not time for power struggles over who sits by whom and other meaningless monitoring, such as who ate what first.

I held family potlucks, a favorite snack day, fruit salad parties where everyone brought their favorite fruit and we cut it all up and made a fruit salad to share. We occasionally acted out the "Stone Soup" story and again shared in the process of cooking, eating, and sharing a meal together.

I planted an edible garden with the children so they could eat what they grew. It's amazing how the interest in beans and other veggies increased when children played a part in the creation of the food! I had cherry tomatoes, green beans, blackberries, and plums available in the yard for the children to eat as they wished.

Have a "teddy bear picnic" outside, or bring lunches on your next walk to the park. My mom used to say that everything tasted better when you ate it outside. I think what really happens when you eat outside is that you are removed from the visual reminders of closets that need to be cleaned, laundry that needs to be folded, around the house fix-it projects, miles of to-do lists, schedules, and calendars with looming deadlines, not to mention the interruptions from dinnertime phone calls and the constant distraction of screens and social media.

Removing yourself from these distractions and going into the calmness and serenity of the outdoors allow you to focus your attention instead on loved ones, family, food, and each delicious bite.

THE sense OF HeaRinG

We don't often listen to each other in our culture. The typical American good-morning greeting goes something like this:

"Hi! How are you?"

"OK!"

"See you later!"

"Bye!"

When most people ask, "How are you?" they don't really want to know; it's just what we say. You experienced this one day when someone asked "How ya doin'?" and you started to actually tell them—you were kind of cranky and had a headache because the dog got out this morning and then you spilled coffee all over your new shirt in the car and then got a flat en route to school . . . and they still say, "OK! See ya later. Bye!"

And you are like, OMG! She wasn't even *listening* to me!

We must practice listening, and not just listening, but *hearing*. There is a difference. It can be hard to really *hear* little children sometimes. It can take them an hour to tell you a story. And when you are trying to watch eleven other children, get Kati to the bus, and change Donnell's diaper, it can be easy to brush them off and say, "Not now." Resist this urge. Stay in the moment and listen. It is hard. Do it anyway!

"Listen! What's that sound?" is a game I play with children to heighten their classification and identification skills but also as a way for children to increase their awareness of the subtle sounds in their environment. Not just the sounds of voices, but a layer deeper, then a layer deeper, until they tell me that they hear the flowers and the wind. The best way to encourage *that* kind of awareness is to practice listening. So we listen to and really *hear* the dog bark, the neighbor's cat purr, and the many sets of wind chimes that grace the back patio. We listen to the "river" (flood channel) behind the house and the helicopters that fly over too. We listen to bees, birds, and construction workers. We clink our glasses at snacktime to say "cheers."

We play music of different styles for listening and dancing. We make our voices LOUD, then we whisper like mice. We use instruments and bells, rattles and gourds, all when playing with sound. We talk through paper towel tubes. I purchased PVC pipe "elbows" that look like huge pieces of elbow macaroni, and the children use them as phones. A workshop participant once told me that a boy in her class uses it to make "announcements." He will say things like, "Mrs. McGuinty, please report to the office. Mrs. McGuinty to the office please!"

On the back fence of the play yard I hung up washboards, pie tins, tin cans, and hubcaps for the children to tap, bang, and make sounds on. I took an old hose cut into three long pieces, a PVC T connector, and three old funnels, duct-taped the whole thing together, and called it "three-way calling." So many things can be used to enhance the children's exploration of sound: tuning forks, large water bottles, cookie cooling trays, slinkys, hubcaps, and even long sections of plastic dryer tube.

We listened to the traffic that went by, including the city buses whose route passed in front of the schoolhouse. We ran out to wave to the drivers, and sometimes they stopped and waved back. We stopped and listened as the sounds from a neighbor's remodeling job drifted into my yard—Bang! Bang! Whirr! Whirr! Beep! Beep! The children hollered out their identifications of the mystery sounds—truck backing up, lawn mower, hammer, saw, faraway train whistle!

And every Wednesday we anxiously anticipated the dumping, crashing sounds that indicated the arrival of the trash man. Have you noticed that preschoolers absolutely adore the trash man? He is like a *superhero* to them! In my community, we had different trash pickups—garbage, recyclables, and yard waste. This, of course, made for three separate visits from every preschooler's favorite community helper. The anticipation of his arrival was almost unbearable. Eventually the sounds outside cued us that he was close, so sand toys got dropped, books were hastily put back on shelves, playdough quickly stuffed back into the bag. We all grabbed hands, ran out front, and waited.

We watched, and we waited. We waited, and we watched. We listened for his brakes and the telltale beep as he backed up. Here he comes! We saw him down the block, coming around the corner, we heard the crashing and the banging of the neighbors' cans being set back down on the sidewalk, until, yes—finally—it was our turn! He jumped out and waved (all three crews knew the routine, so I figure someone circulated a memo), then he dumped everything into the container on the front of the truck and always waited until we were all watching before he dumped the big container over the top and into the big bin hidden inside the belly of the truck. Then he hopped back in, waved good-bye, and tooted his horn as he moved on down the street.

Some children got so worked up at this juncture they could barely contain themselves, jumping up and down, arms raised high over their heads, screaming and clapping! Inside we went to anxiously await the second and third visit. Some children were so excited, they were squirming and dancing, wiggling, screaming, clapping, and just shaking with excitement. I don't know what it's about, but they got *crazy* and all worked up!

Many teachers do the same thing when the UPS man comes.

THE SENSE OF SIGHT

In her previously mentioned book, sense expert Diane Ackerman offers that abstract thinking might have evolved from the elaborate struggle of our eyes to make sense of what they saw. She also points out that 70 percent of the body's sense receptors cluster in the eyes; therefore, it is mainly through *seeing* the world that we appreciate it and understand it.

We must take measures to ensure that classrooms are visually *pleasing*, not visually *overwhelming*. Avoid cutesy, cartoony posters. Instead invest in reprints of quality pieces of art. Better yet, decorate the classroom with the children's art! I have a handful of things that I will not compromise on when it comes to my work with children and families. Saying *no way* to commercialized images is one of them. Therefore, this means no Barney, no Dora, no Bob the Builder, no Sesame Street. And, brace yourself, no Disney. No commercialized stuff in my classroom. Children get enough of that elsewhere, so when they are in my classroom, they get a break from it. It's not a judgment call; it's being mindful of providing a *balance*. I cannot control what happens when they leave the building. I can choose to not contribute to the onslaught of commercialized images they are regularly exposed to. Many of these images, shows, and products exist for no reason other than for toddlers to become loyal, brand-specific shoppers. I heard once (sorry, no actual reference here) that marketing experts can actually project out a child's spending habits as a grown-up *by the age of two* based on the amount of media images the child received daily based on the ZIP code they grew up in. That's scary.

Be aware of the colors in the room too! Somewhere along the way we bought into the idea (myth) that school walls, fixtures, and furniture need to be RED, YELLOW, AND BLUE. No no no! Not always true. I have walked into so many rooms that scream "PRIMARY COLORS ARE USED HERE!" These intense blue, yellow, and red rooms are often both harsh to look at and even painful to the eyes. Walk into a room with lots of red, bright yellow, and dark blue and then into one with soft greens, pastel purples, and light blues. The second room will instantaneously provide a much more calming and peaceful atmosphere. I suggest using pastels, neutral colors, and natural shades. And I would always choose wood over plastic!

I have a friend who painted one wall of the children's playroom red. The children became louder and more aggressive within the week. After the wall was painted a more neutral color, the children's behaviors went back to "normal." I have another friend who shared that her school received some donated carpet, so they put it in the nap room. However, it was *red* carpet! Within three days the children stopped napping. Red is a very energetic color, and it can often bring out aggressiveness in people. It is worth the time and effort to investigate colors and their different emotional, psychological, and physiological impact when decorating rooms where children (and teachers) will be spending a considerable amount of time.

Take the time and make the effort to point out and pay attention to the minor details and minuscule wonders within a child's world. I hired one teacher on the spot when she flopped herself down on her belly right next to the children and spent the next ten minutes silently watching ants crawl through cracks in the sidewalk. Had she flopped down and started chattering incessantly about the ants, saying, "Let's count them," and "I wonder what they are doing," I don't know if I would have been so quick to offer her a job right then. There is just as much talent in knowing when to talk about what you are seeing, how to use descriptive language, and extend the observation with words as there is in knowing when to just shut up.

It took me a long time to learn how to be comfortable with silence and how to embrace stillness. I thought I always had to say something or make a comment. It took a lot of practice to give myself permission to simply observe and not feel the need to look look look and then make a comment. In another lecture I attended, author and educator Alfie Kohn reminded the audience that "terrific teachers have teeth marks on their tongues." There is power in quiet.

Notice and discuss what happens to rain puddles after the sun comes out from behind the clouds. Follow the cricket that just hopped into the room. Watch the birds at the feeders outside. Look at the ants on the floor. Begin observing differences and subtle nuances within your environment. Observe out loud what, *to you,* might seem obvious—someone might have missed something.

As children get older, you can begin to observe more detailed things, such as the differences between hard-boiled eggs and raw eggs, ice and water, or primary colors mixing to make secondary colors. Point out opposites, and give children concrete examples to attach to observations of hot and cold, wet and dry, fast and slow.

Observe and discuss what happens to eggs in salt water and eggs in tap water. What happens when you

* put rock salt on ice?

* mix flour and water?

* pour vinegar into a pie tin filled with baking soda?

* drop a pinecone into a tub of water?

What happens? What do you see? What do you hear? What do you smell? What do you feel?

Time, patience, and awareness will turn a superficial exploration of a few textured carpet squares and baby food jars filled with stale, leftover spices during a My Five Senses Week to a lifelong appreciation of the sights, smells, textures, tastes, and sounds available to us when we see the value in pausing to observe them.

 ## THE IMPORTANCE OF OBSERVING: A REVIEW

1. Making more time to observe means increasing the number of opportunities we provide for children to be engaged with *all* their senses instead of focusing on only one or two.

2. Make sure "observing" isn't reduced to a checklist of the five senses! Smell this: check! Touch this: check!

3. Set aside time to show the importance of noticing/observing (smelling, hearing, etc.) what is happening in the world around us.

4. Reducing observing to Five Senses Week might be rather limiting. Instead consider small ways each day to connect children to their senses to facilitate the development of awareness.

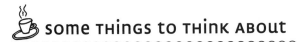

some THiNGS to THiNK ABOUt

1. Are we making enough time for deeper levels of awareness and observation?

2. Am I stuck in the My Five Senses approach?

3. What can we do to increase opportunity for tasting? listening? touching? smelling? seeing?

4. How am I working on embracing the power of silence?

5. What do I smell immediately upon entering my school?

6. My classroom?

7. My family child care space?

8. The playroom?

9. How can I make it more pleasant?

10. How might I make my environment more visually pleasing?

11. What decorates the walls?

12. Might this need to be modified?

13. Do we have enough time in the day to make a point of noticing (hearing, seeing, experiencing) the things around us?

14. How does making time to OBSERVE each day meet the child's cognitive, language/literacy, social/emotional, and physical developmental needs?

15. What steps can I take to be more confident when pointing out these developmental connections to parents? colleagues? naysayers?

16. What is one thing I can do Monday to begin making more time each day for observing?

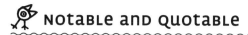

NOTABLE AND QUOTABLE

When we give perfume to someone, we give them liquid memory.

—Diane Ackerman, *A Natural History of the Senses*

If you want to do something good for a child . . . give him an environment where he can touch things as much as he wants.

—Buckminster Fuller, *Buckminster Fuller to Children of Earth*

All knowledge begins in observation.

—Robert and Michèle Root-Bernstein, *Sparks of Genius*

If your knack for observation is not skillful enough to permit you to sketch a man falling out a window during the time it takes him to fall from the 5th story to the ground, you will never produce monumental work.

—Eugène Delacroix, artist

Children marvel at things adults find ordinary, messy, or even boring. From a child's point of view, there are so many things to look at, hold, rub, taste, and smell.

—Deb Curtis and Margie Carter, *The Art of Awareness* (2nd edition)

15

Make Time Each Day to . . . READ

"LOOK LOOK LOOK! *Ann Likes Red!*"
"I remember this one, oh and *Mog the Forgetful Cat!*"
"This one was my *favorite!*"
"Here's *Eighteen Cousins* and even *Miss Suzy!*"
"And look—*Mike Mulligan!*"

You'd have thought that the five of us were preschool children on our first field trip to the library, not young adults helping our parents pack. Although we all had been summoned to the house to help Mom and Dad move, my brothers, sister, and I spent more time rummaging *through* boxes than actually packing and moving them.

Sitting in the living room with piles of books around us on the floor and heaped in our laps, we flipped through pages, recited favorite passages, and shared the pictures with each other like we were looking at them for the first time. We shared our memories that surrounded the books—where we read them, who the books were presents from, specific passages that made us feel scared or happy. We found pages that had been ripped out in long-forgotten fits of anger and overall rediscovered just how much, as children, we identified with the characters. We even went so far as to think we *were* the characters in some of the stories.

Heavy sighs coming from our tired, hard-working parents, along with glances over glasses and gazes from around corners were giving us nonverbal cues to leave the books alone, put them back in the boxes, and get back to the task at hand! Yet we kept reading!

When Mom came in to finally shoo us off couches and out of chairs, we pleaded with her to let us take our favorites with us to our own houses, but to no avail! The books of our past were going to the new house, where they would be ready and waiting for the (at that time) nonexistent grandchildren. We whined and complained so much you'd have thought we were stubborn children in the midst of a tantrum! We resumed packing but not before hiding a few favorites in purses and backpacks. No one wanted to leave the memories and history behind.

Perhaps it's safe to say that, like the songs we learned when we were little, the books that were read to us remain in our hearts and memories too. I've been in the middle of reading storybooks to audience members at workshops when I've seen waitstaff and busboys sit down to listen. One time a guy said, "I haven't heard that one [it was *Where the Wild Things Are*] since I was little. I forgot how great it was!"

But to create these memories, we again find ourselves needing *time*. How about lap time, story time, cuddle time, snacktime, outdoor time, bedtime, and lunchtime? Those are all good times to plop in a storybook. Simply having a book center in the classroom is not promoting a love of reading, especially when, as was the case of a school I once visited, the book center contained nothing but copies of *Glamour* magazine.

In addition to creating a book center with cozy pillows and filled with high-quality picture books, we must read to children. Bev Bos says we must, "Read! Read! Read! Until you think your lips are going to fall off, and then, read one more!" And we must read "good" books. While children are perfectly capable of self-selecting books from the shelf, it is up to us to make sure the choices provided are good ones. And just what makes a "good" book? In *Dear Mem Fox, I Have Read All Your Books Even the Pathetic Ones*, acclaimed children's author Mem Fox says, "good books have as much to do with the effect they have on the reader as with any other criterion. If we don't laugh, gasp, howl, block our ears, sigh, vomit, giggle, curl our toes, empathize, sympathize, feel pain, weep or shiver during the reading of a picture book, then surely the writer has wasted our time, our money and our precious, precious trees" (149). At the end of this chapter, I have included a list of some of my favorite books and authors for you.

Teachers and parents are usually well aware of the classic children's books that have withstood the test of time, and you probably already have those at home and in the classroom. Broaden your repertoire and have a wide variety of books available: nonfiction, poetry, short stories, fairy tales, books with and without pictures, coffee-table photography books, how-to books, classic chapter books, myths, nursery rhymes . . . the list is endless! The lesson is to pay attention to the children's interests—not just your own—when selecting books.

For teachers who barely make enough money to live on, it can be tempting to purchase the bucket of books we find at a garage sale—cheap and often of poor quality, ripped and torn. We might wonder if it's worth the money spent on hardback books if "all the children do is rip them." Yet what kind of messages are we sending if our book centers are filled with books that are ripped and have torn pages? How can we expect children to not rip them if those are the only kinds of books we are offering them? If we *expect* that the children will rip books, they will. If, however, we teach them how to handle books, treat them with care, put them away when finished, and point out rips, tears, and pages in need of repair so helpful grown-up hands can fix them, we are teaching skills that will encourage not only the love of books but the respect of them as well.

I once worked as a substitute in a classroom where the last few pages of a certain book were missing. Someone had torn them out, and the book had never been mended or replaced. I brought in my own copy of this particular book so the children could see the missing pictures and hear how the story ended—but they wanted nothing to do with it! When we read through my copy, eventually getting to the page where theirs had been torn, they wanted to go no further and insisted that *that* was the end of the book!

Make the investment, and purchase good books. Two or three hardback favorites are better than a box filled with hundreds of ripped and torn commercialized books. Also, buy a big, thick roll of clear packing tape so that when the books get ripped and torn (which they will), the children can assist you as you fix them. There is no better way to model the value and importance of books.

I was subbing another time, and the note left for me by the teacher indicated that the "good books" were to be kept in the cupboard and were for "teacher hands only." Children were allowed to look only at the books in the book center. Upon examining the books in the center, I was disgusted. Ripped, torn, old stories, horrible pictures, arrg! My message to you: put the "good books" out and take responsibility for showing children how to use them!

Babies need chubby board books with pictures of real objects in them, along with books that encourage their involvement, like *Pat the Bunny*. Be sure the baby's book basket also includes board book reprints of classics such as *Goodnight Moon* and *Brown Bear, Brown Bear, What Do You See?* Even though babies are not yet verbal and might not *appear* interested (yet), reading to a baby early on sets the stage for an enjoyment of stories as they grow up and begins the ritual of appreciating, listening, looking, and cuddling up with a book. It also assists the adults in getting in the habit of reading with children as often as possible!

For preschoolers, provide engaging books that promote questions and discussions. Read aloud to children often, and allow them to read to each other too. Remember what we learned about children needing to talk out loud to process their thoughts? A group of preschoolers reading out loud on the carpet both to themselves and each other disturbs no one except the teacher who is demanding a quiet classroom.

Provide books with lush, detailed pictures and a meaningful story line, not something designed to be preachy or teachy. You want to find stories that promote questions and discussions immediately on page one. Older toddlers and preschoolers will begin to sit for longer story times; be sure to have both paperback and hardbound editions of classics, and multiple copies of classroom favorites. If the children don't get involved, don't ask questions, and don't seem interested in the book being read, by all means put it down and pick a different one. There is no hard-and-fast rule that says you must finish a book just because you started it! *Our goal is not "to get to the end of the book"!* The purpose of reading is not solely to finish the book but also to enjoy great stories by great authors. I have been known to start a story for children, only to still be on page one after fifteen minutes because everyone had something to say about the picture or the story! Set aside the self-induced pressure of "needing to finish the book." If you are simply reading to hurry up, turn the page, and finish the book, you miss out on sharing an amazing experience with the children.

If you are tired, angry, in a bad mood, or simply otherwise grouchy, don't take it out on a book! Ask the child to read to you, take a minute to calm down. Then read another book to them. Record yourself reading your children's favorite book. Five times in a row. Then have a friend read the book. Five times in a row. Then Dad and Grandma too. This recording might prove to be a lifesaver on that one day when you are extra tired and don't want to read, for when you are absent, or when your child just wants something different. Before she died, my grandma recorded herself reading all our favorite books to us. My sister's favorite is Grandma's rendition of *The Jolly Postman*. Grandma even changed up her voice for all the letters the postman delivered. Treasures such as these are priceless. Make some for your family and classroom.

Always read a book on your own before reading it to a group of children. From this, you can use Mem Fox's criteria to see if it is a "good book," develop a feeling for the characters and the story line, and determine whether it is appropriate for your age group.

A quality book corner will include easy books, just-right books, and books that are a wee bit challenging. This way, when children are ready for something a little more complex, it is already on hand for their enjoyment. I also read aloud stories that do not have any pictures. I do this so that children can practice making their own pictures in their heads! I tell stories from the top of my head and also do visualizations with the children. I tell the children, "I'm going to tell you a story. See if you can make the pictures appear in your head!" I see this as good practice for children who are growing up in a media-drenched culture where all of their images are being created for them!

Books are read inside, outside, up in trees, and under them. Books are read on swings and before naptime, and there are books available in the bathrooms. Books are brought on neighborhood walks to the park and on picnics too. Books are not mandated to stay in the book area. Family-related stories are in the dress-up center and home living. Building, construction, and transportation books are added to the block corner. Time is carved out for one-on-one reading with children as well as planned group story times. Don't reserve reading only for group time or circle time! Reading should be happening all day long!

Feel free to alter the names in the story by substituting the name(s) of children or adults in the class for characters in the story. Give yourself permission to play with the words in the story too. I once spent an entire circle time with a group of four-year-olds doing nothing but substituting words in the title of *The Little Mouse, the Red Ripe Strawberry, and the Big Hungry Bear*. The children were roaring with laughter, rolling on the carpet and doubled over with glee. They were hollering out their own suggestions too. After some time, we all decided that our favorite was *The Little Boy, the Red Ripe Banana, and the Big Hungry Belly Button!* Hushing and shushing their joyful outbursts in order to "read the book" would have squashed the use of descriptive language, silenced the laughter, and destroyed the experience completely. We eventually got around to reading the book all the way through, and it quickly became a popular favorite. Each time we would pull it off the shelf for group time, the children would say, "Remember the day we made up all those words?"

I encourage you to avoid commercialized books that reinforce television viewing and turn preschoolers into consumers. Do you really need books that are nothing more than glorified commercials and advertisements for movies and products?

Never under any circumstances tell a child who might be in trouble to "Go sit down and read a book" or to "Go sit in the book corner." True, the book corner might be a quiet area that is conducive to calming down, but in reality you are *linking being in trouble with reading*. It's not a positive association. In addition, a child who is worked up and out of control is in no condition to sit independently and read a book. (And we wonder why the pages get ripped?) Can *you* concentrate on reading when you are mad, angry, or upset? Of course not! A better suggestion might be to go *with* this child to the rocking chair, and while holding him on your lap, spend some time together. Classrooms that use writing as punishment need to question the effectiveness of this practice too. Demanding children to write a sentence a hundred times or to write on the board what they will not do anymore does nothing but kill their desire to write *anything*. Please be mindful of not linking reading and writing to any form of punishment.

If you really want your children to be excited about reading, then make sure they see you reading too! Do the children ever see you reading a book? Or do they see you focused on screens and other devices? It's no secret that modern technology coupled with busy schedules can keep us away from books, stories, and family reading nights. Remember that we teach children what is valuable by the way they see us spending our own time. Turn off the TV, shut off the computer, stop answering the phone, and permit your children to see you engrossed in a book!

In their book *Reading Begins at Home*, authors Dorothy Butler and Marie Clay tell a story about a five-year-old girl who snatched a book from her father and with her eyes fixed with frustration and determination, passionately demanded, "Tell me what it is! Tell me what it says! Read it to me!" She was certain it must be fascinating because he had not taken his eyes off it for an hour!

By linking stories to experiences, we can make even a bigger impact. For example, when reading *Blueberries for Sal*, have real blueberries available to eat. The house across the street from our schoolhouse went through a complete remodeling. There were bulldozers and dump trucks in front of the house for weeks! We linked this experience up with many books that expanded on what the children were actually witnessing in the front yard! When Ian came back to school from his camping trip announcing he had seen a bear (they really had), we found a resurgence of interest in all our bear-oriented books! Books and experience definitely go hand in hand!

It is also to our advantage if we learn the *art* of reading stories to children. I have had countless teachers tell me that they don't understand why the children in their class refuse to come to story time. Then I listen to these teachers reading a story. Let me put it this way: a flat, garbled, soft-spoken, boring, monotone recitation of *Where the Wild Things Are* does *not* capture the emotion of the story! Quick-paced, hurry-up-and-get-to-the-end readings of *The Napping House* or *The Very Hungry Caterpillar* that are broken up only by the teacher's frazzled and annoyed commands of "Sit still!" "Get on your bottom!" "Crisscross applesauce!" "One, two, three! Eyes on me!" and "SHHHHHH!! I'm reading!" ruin the flavor of the story and the overall purpose of gathering to read the story in the first place. You come together to read a story and to experience a good book. Here's a suggestion: Record yourself reading, and then listen to it. How does it sound? How about the pitch? Is there a natural intonation to your speech—a moving up and down pattern? Do you use volume for emphasis, calling on both loud and quiet to add flavor to the story, or is it monotone? Are you reading too fast or maybe too slow? Do you vary the speed? When we become better at reading, the children become better at listening.

One of the hardest jobs I have had is attempting to convince parents and teachers that when it comes to strengthening the foundation of reading, all they really need is twenty minutes of reading time and a library card. Even if you can afford to purchase a collection of books for your classroom or child care program, you and the children will still benefit from having a library card. Visit the library at your child's school, support your local community library, attend story time, get to know the librarians, and demand the continued purchase of books. Many school libraries are being turned into computer labs, book-purchasing budgets are being cut to purchase technology equipment, and librarians are being replaced with "information specialists." Let's make sure our libraries maintain a nice balance of people, technology, and BOOKS.

The library is a valuable community resource, and I encourage you to visit it with the children as often as possible. The library houses so much more than books. It holds information, keys to history, past and present knowledge, passports to adventures, and, most of all, people. Not just people who know just what we're looking for and who can suggest something appropriate, but also people who assist us with research reports and help us master the new catalog. There are other people too—community members, neighbors, lonely people, happy people, children, and families, who, as different as they might look and be, share in the love of reading and believe in the power of books.

So whether you get books from garage sales, the library, or a bookstore, take the time to make sure they are books that are relevant and meaningful to the children you plan on sharing them with. Read to the children *every single day*, have books all around the house and classroom, and let children see you reading too. If you want children to read, read to them. It's as simple as that!

A VERY SHORT LIST OF MY FAVORITE CHILDREN'S PICTURE BOOKS

Abiyoyo by Pete Seeger

Alexander and the Terrible, Horrible, No Good, Very Bad Day by Judith Viorst

Animals Should Definitely Not Wear Clothing by Judi Barrett

Bark, George by Jules Feiffer

Blueberries for Sal by Robert McCloskey

Borreguita and the Coyote by Verna Aardema

Brown Bear, Brown Bear, What Do You See? by Bill Martin Jr. and Eric Carle

Caps for Sale by Esphyr Slobodkina

Catch the Baby! by Lee Kingman

Chicka Chicka Boom Boom by Bill Martin Jr. and John Archambault

The Cinder-Eyed Cats by Eric Rohmann

Clay Boy by Mirra Ginsburg

Clip-Clop by Nicola Smee

Corduroy by Don Freeman

Darkness by Mildred Pitts Walter

Don't Fidget a Feather! by Erica Silverman

Dooly and the Snortsnoot by Jack Kent

Each Peach Pear Plum by Janet and Allan Ahlberg

Emma's Eggs by Margriet Ruurs

The Giant Jam Sandwich by John Vernon Lord

Good Dog, Carl by Alexandra Day

Good Night, Gorilla by Peggy Rathmann

Goodnight Moon by Margaret Wise Brown

Gotcha! by Gail Jorgensen

Happy Birth Day! by Robie Harris

How the Sun Was Brought Back to the Sky by Mirra Ginsburg

How to Heal a Broken Wing by Bob Graham

I Love You the Purplest by Barbara Joosse

I Stink! by Kate and Jim McMullan

If . . . by Sarah Perry

Imogene's Antlers by David Small

Ira Sleeps Over by Bernard Waber

It Looked Like Spilt Milk by Charles Shaw

It's the Bear! by Jez Alborough

Leo the Late Bloomer by Robert Kraus

Little Blue and Little Yellow by Leo Lionni

The Little House by Virginia Lee Burton

The Little Mouse, the Red Ripe Strawberry, and the Big Hungry Bear by Don and Audrey Wood

The Little Old Lady Who Was Not Afraid of Anything by Linda Williams

Llama Llama Red Pajama by Anna Dewdney

Llama Llama Mad at Mama by Anna Dewdney

Madeline by Ludwig Bemelmans

The Magic Quilt by Clair Thompson

Mama Zooms by Jane Cowen-Fletcher

Mike Mulligan and His Steam Shovel by Virginia Lee Burton

Monster Goose by Judy Sierra

Monster Mama by Liz Rosenberg

"More More More," Said the Baby by Vera Williams

Mortimer by Robert Munsch

Murmel, Murmel, Murmel by Robert Munsch

My Daddy by Susan Paradis

My Dog Rosie by Isabelle Harper

The Napping House by Audrey and Don Wood

Night Driving by John Coy

No, David! by David Shannon

Our Granny by Margaret Wild

Owl Babies by Martin Waddell

Owl Moon by Jane Yolen

The Pout-Pout Fish by Deborah Diesen

Purple, Green and Yellow by Robert Munsch

Quick as a Cricket by Audrey Wood

The Relatives Came by Cynthia Rylant

Roxaboxen by Alice McLerran

The Snowy Day by Ezra Jack Keats

Somebody and the Three Blairs by Marilyn Tolhurst

Sophie by Mem Fox

A Special Kind of Love by Stephen Michael King

Spoon by Amy Krouse Rosenthal

Stephanie's Ponytail by Robert Munsch

Thomas' Snowsuit by Robert Munsch

Tikki Tikki Tembo by Arlene Mosel

Time Flies by Eric Rohmann

Tough Boris by Mem Fox

Tuesday by David Wiesner

The Very Hungry Caterpillar by Eric Carle

Where the Wild Things Are by Maurice Sendak

Wolf's Coming! by Joe Kulka

A VERY SMALL LIST OF MY FAVORITE CLASSIC CHAPTER BOOKS

Alice's Adventures in Wonderland by Lewis Carroll

Black Beauty by Anna Sewell

Bridge to Terabithia by Katherine Paterson

Catherine, Called Birdy by Karen Cushman

Charlotte's Web by E. B. White

Chitty Chitty Bang Bang: The Magical Car by Ian Fleming

The Family under the Bridge by Natalie Savage Carlson and Garth Williams

The Good Earth by Pearl S. Buck

Jim the Boy by Tony Earley

Johnny Tremain by Esther Hoskins Forbes

Little House on the Prairie (series) by Laura Ingalls Wilder

Mr. Popper's Penguins by Richard Atwater and Florence Atwater

National Velvet by Enid Bagnold

Peter Rabbit (series) by Beatrix Potter

Roll of Thunder, Hear My Cry by Mildred D. Taylor

The Secret Garden by Frances Hodgson Burnett

The Story of Babar: The Little Elephant (and others in the series) by Jean De Brunhoff

Stuart Little by E. B. White

The Swiss Family Robinson by Johann David Wyss

The Trumpet of the Swan by E. B. White

Tuck Everlasting by Natalie Babbit

The Witch of Blackbird Pond by Elizabeth George Speare

A Wrinkle in Time (series) Madeleine L'Engle

And every book written by Roald Dahl

THE IMPORTANCE OF READING: A REVIEW

1. Children who grow up to be readers are children who have been read to.

2. Our goal is not to "get to the end of the book" but rather to instill of love of reading and of stories.

3. Change up the character names and even the title to be more playful or expressive.

4. It is OK for children to interrupt the story with questions and comments.

5. It is not required to buy lots of books; instead, use the library!

6. Books that were read to you as a child are powerful bridges between you, your past, and the children you care for and teach.

 ## SOME THINGS TO THINK ABOUT

1. Am I making enough time for reading stories?

2. Do I have "good books" available?

3. How much reading am I doing on my own time?

4. Am I ready to record myself while reading to children and use what I hear as feedback for making changes to how I read to children?

5. Do I have someone I could process the outcome with?

6. What books do I remember from my childhood?

7. Who read to me when I was little?

8. Were books a priority in my home growing up?

9. How has that influenced the role of books and reading in my classroom?

10. While making time to READ each day obviously connects to a child's language and literacy development, do you see any connection to cognitive, social/emotional, and physical development?

11. What steps can I take to be more confident when pointing out these developmental connections to parents? colleagues? naysayers?

12. What is one thing I can do Monday to begin making more time each day to read?

NOTABLE AND QUOTABLE

No book is really worth reading at the age of ten when not equally— and often far more—worth reading at the age of fifty.

—C. S. Lewis

The best time to start reading aloud to a baby is the day it is born.

—Mem Fox

If you want your children to be intelligent, read them fairy tales. If you want them to be more intelligent, read them more fairy tales.

—Albert Einstein

Read, read, read, read, and, when you think your lips are going to fall off, read one more!

—Bev Bos

16

Make Time Each Day to . . . PLAY

WHEN I PRESENT this material in workshops, I tell the audience that "play" is not a separate seventh thing within the foundation of children's learning, but it is what holds everything together. I have said this a few times throughout the book and will say it again: *Playing is the cement that holds the foundation together.* When the foundation is strong, the house of higher learning, the house of "academics," as it were, can be built on top of it. But at the base of it all is *play*. Everything I have talked about up until now has been grounded in play—creating is playing, moving is playing, singing is playing, discussing is playing, observing is playing, and reading is playing. Learning is playing, and playing is learning. Playful learning is how children get ready for school.

It is important to point out that adults and children have different definitions of play. Play to an adult might be to engage in a fun activity that has a tangible result or end product, such as sewing a dress, making a quilt, planting a garden, refinishing a boat, playing a softball game, running a marathon, or building a shed. The way a child wants to play is often very different from what parents or teachers might think is best. To some adults, child play appears disconnected, having no readily observable focus or goals, and no real end product.

Child play is filled with loose parts, bits and pieces, sticks, balls, rocks, snails, dolls, mud, water, bikes, and skateboards. There is quite a bit of milling around. There is much emphasis on the gathering of things and, oftentimes, long periods of time talking about the "rules" of the game. And while the grown-ups are standing around, anxiously waiting for the play to start, they do not see that it has already begun. The planning of the play and the setting of the stage are vital parts of the play. Deciding who gets the blue horse, who will be the baby kitty, who will push the red truck, and who will get the green shovel are all essential pieces of the playing puzzle. Many early childhood professionals have stated that this discussion and deciding are actually more important than "playing." Antsy grown-up onlookers who are anxious for the roads to be built, the block tower to be created, and the tea party to begin get frustrated because they have forgotten that play is a process, not just an outcome.

Bev Bos has frequently said that most grown-ups have childhood amnesia! We have forgotten what it is like to be little, so we inadvertently redirect, shut off, and stifle play because we think that we should be *teaching*. We must pause to remember that *play is a very intellectual activity overflowing with opportunities for problem solving and creativity*. To really begin believing and understanding this, though, we must first allow ourselves to remember what it was like when we were children. Here are some questions to get you started. Take the time to answer them:

- ✿ How did you play when you were little?
- ✿ Where did you play?
- ✿ What did you do?
- ✿ Who was with you?
- ✿ How did you spend those lazy summer days?
- ✿ What did you do each day after school?
- ✿ Where were the grown-ups?
- ✿ How old were the other children you played with?

* How did you know when it was time to come home?

* What did you do on Saturdays?

* What did you do on Sundays?

I call this process getting back to the "pre"—stopping for a minute and thinking about what it was like *before* we grew up and decided we had the answers to everything. Until we allow ourselves to begin the process of remembering, we will continue to tell children to "Stop!" or "Come over here and do something else!" and we will continue to be so very concerned and worried that they aren't *doing* anything, when in fact they are *doing* a lot, we have just forgotten what it is. Here are some more questions to consider:

* What was it like to see a bubble for the first time?

* Can you remember when you finally reached the pedals on your new bicycle?

* Did you ever eat paste?

* What was your feeling when you made it all the way across the monkey bars for the first time?

* Do you recall the feel of squishing playdough or clay the first time?

* How about making a mud pie?

* Do you remember squeezing glue on your hands and waiting for it to dry so you could peel it off?

When we allow ourselves to remember, we become better teachers, parents, and educators. When we reconnect with the power of play, we realize the importance of making time for it. George Bernard Shaw reportedly said that "we don't stop playing because we grow old, we grow old because we stop playing." With so many hours spent in organized activities, such as piano lessons, gymnastics, soccer, and dance class, along with the constant distraction of technology, screens, and social media, we might often find ourselves asking, "Where has all the play time gone?"

Just because *we* are overworked, tired, overscheduled, and stressed doesn't mean we must pass these behaviors on to our children. On one of my travels I met a woman who had a day planner for her four-year-old in order to keep track of her child's extracurricular activities. Formal scheduled playdates with friends were wedged in between violin lessons, dance class, birthday parties, soccer games, computer classes, and (I could only assume) her shrink.

Time is necessary for meaningful play. When children are shuffled from one activity to the next simply because that is what the schedule says it's time to do, no one is receiving the full benefit of the experience. Many preschools chop up the day into manageable twenty-minute time blocks. Twenty minutes is not enough time for anything! It takes some children a good ten minutes just to choose what activity they want to do when they come to school each morning! So they spend ten minutes choosing, five minutes playing, and another five minutes being told that it's time to clean up! "Clean up?" they say. "Clean up? I haven't even *done* anything yet!"

And after awhile, if this pattern is allowed to continue, guess what happens? *They stop playing.* One group of children I was working with told me, "Miss Lisa, we used to build big block towers, but it was always time to put them away." The children realized there was never enough time anyway, so why bother?

Why bother, indeed. If it is always time to put it away, why bother taking it off the shelf? If there is no time to paint, why bother purchasing an easel? If there is no time to go outside, why bother having bikes? If there is no time for singing, why bother making musical instruments? If there is no time for talking, why bother coming together as a group? If there is not time for observing, why bother noticing anything? If there is no time for reading, why bother writing new stories? If there is no time for playing . . . You get the idea.

If there is no time for playing, our house of higher learning is going to crumble to the ground. Playing is the cement that holds our foundation of creating, moving, singing, discussing, observing, and reading together, and cement needs time to set so the foundation can be solid and sturdy. The foundation needs to be strong because it is going to support the house of higher learning. The cycle needs both components to be complete. *We must stop demanding houses where there are no foundations!*

When children are playing with blocks, they are learning about *balance* as they stack them, about *shapes* as they figure out the ones they need for their tower, about *estimating* as they figure out how many more blocks are needed for their house. They *measure* as they determine the length of the road for their cars, and they learn about *gravity* when it all comes crashing down. They learn *patience* when it doesn't turn out right the first time, and *persistence* when they pick up the pieces to start all over again. They explore *math* concepts as they fit six small squares together to make one big rectangle and begin to experiment with *elements of design* when adding other available "things," such as fabric, thread spools, milk caps, and corks to their wooden towers.

When dressing up and playing in the house corner, they are learning about manners, social roles, and valuable communication skills. They are expanding their creativity while pretending and enhancing their imaginations.

When painting, they are working through the stages of scribbling, experimenting with color and design, mixing primary colors to make secondary ones, learning about shape placement, and engaging in self-expression.

When doing puzzles, they are solving problems, learning to concentrate, figuring out spatial relationships as they fit pieces together, and learning to see a whole from its parts.

When splashing in water, they are learning about evaporation and absorption, as well as mastering the small-motor skills necessary for pouring without spilling.

When doing basic science experiments, they are learning about cause and effect, properties of water, density, how to make comparisons, understanding opposites, as well as being able to experience messy, squishy, drippy materials in an environment suitable for exploration.

When in the sandbox, they are measuring, scooping, discovering saturation points, learning about irrigation when draining puddles after a rainstorm, learning how to cooperate, as well as having time for problem solving and sharing practice.

When running around, chasing each other, climbing trees and rocks, they are strengthening their bodies and mastering large-motor skills, which will in turn support the small-motor skill development that is necessary for eventually holding pencils and crayons.

When singing and exploring musical instruments, children are learning about sounds. They are exploring rhythm and patterns—all of which will assist them later on as they begin to study math. In addition, music connects children to their families and communities on a social level through the continuation of songs and other cultural traditions.

When discussing and observing, children are using their senses to unlock the beauty of the world and acquiring the necessary skills to speak with others about what they are experiencing. Children realize they can learn from others in order to broaden their own horizons and that conversation is a give-and-take process. Discussion plants the seeds of problem solving and teaches children that they have the power to deal with conflict with their words, not their fists. Developing and nurturing social and emotional skills are truly how we work to "get children ready for school."

When reading, children are learning the importance of books. They are cultivating an understanding of their language. They are being exposed to words, concepts, and ideas that will link back to their own lives, thus strengthening the connection between experience and books. If our claims of wanting to raise a generation of readers are true, children must be read to, and they must see us reading too.

Play is not mindless, meaningless self-amusement. Yet we constantly find ourselves having to defend the value and importance of play in the lives of children. At what point will we no longer have to constantly justify play by attaching the actions we see in play to cognitive concepts or rationalized skills that somehow make play more acceptable to the watchful, often judgmental eyes of parents, center directors, teachers, superintendents, policy makers, and most grown-ups in general?

IF we Link it to a standard, THen can we Let THem PLay?

Sometimes we get so caught up in the whirlwind of needing to know what children are *doing* when they are playing that we forget the fact that sometimes it is OK to play simply for the sheer fun of it. It has been said that the very existence of *research* about play indicates that we are a very serious society capable of taking the fun out of almost anything. Play is important even when it does not *look like* anything! All play is essential to the complete development of our children, not just the play that can be linked back to a standard. What do I mean by this? I mean that creating ooblick, the mixture of cornstarch and water, simply for the sake of making ooblick is a valuable experience worthy of exploration! The fact that it is also introducing concepts such as action and reaction, cause and effect, evaporation and absorption and giving a very basic knowledge of the creation of non-Newtonian fluids (a substance that has the properties of a solid and a liquid at the same time) are all bonus points! Extra credit! Ooblick is an amazing sensorial experience that activates socialization as children talk about how it feels when it drips down their arms, encourages problem solving, measuring, and estimation as they figure out just how much water makes the "perfect batch," and develops small-motor skills as they squeeze and squish it with their hands and fingers.

To do ooblick only because it meets the twice-a-week curriculum requirement to expose the children to chemistry limits the experience for all who are involved. Teachers are then doing it only to meet a requirement, and children are provided only the allotted time to experience it. Why bother?

Yes, professional educators, family child care providers, and preschool teachers need to be able to articulate the learning that is happening when these experiences are provided *but not at the expense of taking the playfulness and fun out of the experience.* Professional educators need to have a working knowledge of the research and literature that supports a play-based teaching philosophy, and when asked, they need to be able to articulate what they know and apply it to the experiences being offered to the children in their programs. Linking it back? Yes. Needing to prove it? No!

The *proving* of the importance of play has already been done. We have years of research that documents the many benefits of play as fostering and encouraging the intellectual, social, emotional, physical, language, and spiritual development of our children. In light of all this existing research, it would seem, then, that our job would be to apply this knowledge in schools and classrooms. Or so it would appear. For many educators, this is just simply not the case. Many educators find themselves in environments where, for whatever reason, it is still necessary for them to *prove* that play is very important.

We should no longer have to defend the value of play in the lives of children! Yet by still being required and expected to justify every action that looks like "play" and not like "learning," we become distracted from our real job of creating engaging environments that meet the developmental needs of children. We spend hours arming ourselves with an arsenal of information so we are ready at a moment's notice for our ongoing battle with the naysayers. We find ourselves constantly on guard, prepared and ready at all times to defend ourselves and prove our point. It can be tiring. It makes us frustrated. It's also rather demeaning.

As professional educators, we earn degrees, participate in extra classes, read journals, have thick studies of child development by our bedside, go to conferences, and spend our own money to enhance the environments we create for the children. We also learn new skills, talk shop at dinner parties (much to the dismay of our significant others), share ideas with colleagues, and make efforts to constantly expand our horizons and our understanding of what we do. How annoying it becomes when we are treated as though we don't know what we are talking about.

At what point will the job we do be valued enough and considered professional enough that when we share our words, statements, discoveries, and insights, they are believed? Not shrugged off, not discounted, and not thought to be just "fluff" (as one parent told me once). When people go to the doctor, they don't demand to see the latest article that supports the diagnosis or the lab report analyzing the new antibiotic that was prescribed. Yet *our* practices in early childhood are constantly questioned, demanding us to be armed with an arsenal of information, ready at a moment's notice to defend the importance of play. Why isn't it accepted that we, as teachers and educators, like doctors, business folk, and scientists, know what we are talking about too?

I had a thought as to *why not* while I was writing this book. I began realizing that the people we run into every day are professionals and experts in their field, whether it be law, medicine, government, business, architecture, interior design, customer service, retail, whatever. They know about their field and make every effort to stay abreast of their area of expertise. When we have questions and need answers about a topic in their profession, we call upon someone like them to assist us because they know things about their field that we don't. They are the experts.

At the same time, we too have chosen to become experts. Our area of expertise, however, is children. *Their children.* Children *are* our profession. By having elected that profession, we have made it our job to know about children, schools, education, activities, stages, developmental issues. We learn all of the stuff that comes along with a major in early childhood education or child development.

Appearing professional and knowing our stuff can mistakenly be interpreted as telling other people how to raise their children. Follow me on this? When contractors know their stuff, they do their job and build a great fence. You love your new fence, and everyone is happy. When chefs know their stuff, they do their job, buy the right ingredients, and prepare a delicious dish. You love your dinner, and everyone is happy. When we educators know our stuff and do our job, we're sometimes told, "Don't tell me how to raise my child." OUCH!

A Dream?

My dream is that someday when we say the children "played today," not only will it bring up images of squished orange piles of playdough pancakes, loopy scribbled circles, story times, and blue and yellow water squirted in the air with turkey basters, but it will automatically be understood to mean lessons in math, language, and science. It will mean that the children were actively involved in creating ideas and exploring environments. I fantasize that the grown-ups will immediately recognize that this means problem solving and the development of shared understandings—all of which were being facilitated by caring professional adults who are *experts* in their field. These experts know what they are talking about and know what they are doing. Until then, I continue to read, write, and collect articles for my own Playful Learning = School Readiness evidence binder.

Years ago I attended a lecture about play in the lives of children by Thomas Armstrong. He made a very interesting comment. He expressed concern that without play, our culture will stop evolving and thus perish. Here is what he had on his overhead:

Experiences + Imagination = Something New

According to Armstrong, the Something New is what continues to move a culture forward. *To cultivate imagination, we need playful, creative thinkers who have been provided time to cultivate these characteristics.*

A college professor I had used to say that everything new is half-familiar. Sounds like Piaget to me! Good programs are programs that build on this idea. They realize children need consistency. Children thrive on repetition while at the same time they benefit from exposure to rich, meaningful, engaging experiences. Good programs provide children with enough time to wallow in experiences, figure things out, and think things through. Good programs hire teachers to serve as facilitators and extenders of the play. They employ adults who deserve to be treated like professionals because they act like a professional, not just because they have enough units.

WHat IS a "GOOD" PROGRam?

Please be aware of the fact that you cannot identify good programs by their names, locations, or affiliations with certain philosophies. The distinction between "nursery school," "preschool," "child care center," and "day care" is nothing more than superficial verbiage.

I have seen bad schools in upper-class neighborhoods and excellent schools in poor ones. I have seen authentic, high-quality Montessori schools, and I have also observed places that claimed affiliation because they "bought all the stuff." I have seen family child care homes where children are cared for by loving professional providers, and other family child cares where car seats filled with babies line the hallway. I have called high-dollar private schools on the phone to inquire about their philosophy and have been told one thing, only to call back a few days later and be told something completely different.

I have met excellent, professional teachers who would lay their lives down for their children, and I have also met the ones who yell at children when they think no one is watching. Both kinds of these teachers are in preschools, family child care homes, elementary schools, public schools, private schools, half-day schools, and full-day schools.

We must pull our heads out of the sand and take our power back. It is our job to make sure the places where children are spending their days are in those children's utmost, highest, and best interest.

Your program's ZIP code, glossy marketing brochures, and streaming live Internet cameras do not guarantee quality. Teachers must take responsibility to ensure their classroom is the best it can be. Administrators must do the same for the school. And I'm talking about the best it can be *for the children you serve*—not simply focusing on what makes it easier for the adults! Owners and directors need to find the balance between the neat and tidy "bottom line" and the not always so neat and tidy job of providing for children and their families. Everyone involved in your program (even if you are a one-person family child care program) can help parents understand what quality looks like. Encourage them to ask questions!

Tell them they can show up *unannounced* at all hours to check you out—drop-off, snack or mealtime, pickup, whenever. Tell parents to beware of any place that makes them call first before showing up. Parents should not put their child in the first place they tour simply because the parents need child care by tomorrow! It might be easier for them, but what about the child?

Help educate parents about what to look for. Explain that there is no guarantee that one program is better than another simply because it's accredited, it has lots of rating stars, their friends like it, it has a good reputation on the mommy blogs, it has a fancy name, or it is in a la-di-da neighborhood. Tell parents about playful learning and how it connects to developmentally appropriate practice. Explain that a quality program (such as *yours*) provides children opportunities to develop and explore *all four* domains of developmentally appropriate practice: cognitive, language and literacy, physical, and social/emotional. Tell parents that any program that emphasizes one domain at the expense of another is not being developmentally appropriate. Show the parents how the children in your program are creating, moving, singing, discussing, observing, reading, and playing. Parents will recognize that your program is a keeper.

It is your responsibility to let parents know that in your program children are not expected to sit still and be quiet 24-7. They won't be doing work sheets or flash cards. Explain that these things are not appropriate expectations for young children. If the parents doubt you, it is time to pull out your binder—you know, the one with PLAYFUL LEARNING = SCHOOL READINESS on the cover. You do have that binder by now, don't you?

Tell parents that they will know a good program when they see it because THEY would want to spend some time there. More often than not, they will be able to identify a good program when they walk in the door. It is noisy. There are teachers on the floor, not standing around. There is child-centered art on the bulletin boards, not twenty identical cows made out of paper plates that the teacher glued together. There are tables with engaging activities on them.

There are children inside and outside. There are no "time-out" chairs, and children are gathered around books and bunnies, not screens. Parents will hear laughter and singing, and they will see smiling faces, both young and old. They will see teachers modeling problem-solving techniques and redirecting when necessary. There will be loose parts, engaging equipment, and readily available materials. It will smell nice and not be overwhelmingly "cute." Parents might see real emotions, because even children have bad days sometimes. There might be tears or angry voices, but there will also be a grown-up nearby, comforting, consoling, holding . . .

You enjoy what you do, and parents can see it in your face. You have created an environment where children can get lost in curiosity and spend their days surrounded by discovery and wonder. When parents come to your program, their heart will feel happy, their breathing will be calm, and their mind will be at ease. They will have found a good place—a quality program.

Environments like yours provide enough time each day for creating, moving, singing, discussing, observing, and reading; children are engaged in playful learning. Places like yours are preparing children for school. Preschool is not a boot camp for kindergarten.

THE IMPORTANCE OF PLAYING: A REVIEW

1. Child play is different from grown-up play.

2. Adults suffer from childhood amnesia.

3. Playing is learning, and learning is playing. To think they aren't the same is encouraging the false dichotomy of playing versus learning.

4. The foundation of play supports the house of higher learning.

some THiNGS to THiNK ABOut

1. Until now had I stopped to think about the amount of time children really need when playing?

2. Am I making enough time for playing?

3. Do we need to have more discussion in our school, center, or home about the importance of play?

4. How did I play when I was little?

5. Who did I play with?

6. Am I suffering from childhood amnesia?

7. What is my understanding of play as "cement" in the context of the Seven Things serving as the foundation of the house of higher learning?

8. Am I able to articulate the importance of play in early childhood environments to those who ask?

9. Is it time to accept the Binder Challenge?

10. Do I really believe in the power of play?

11. Identify ten "play scenarios" that happened in the past week. Brainstorm all the ways this PLAYING contributed to a child's cognitive, language/literacy, social/emotional, and physical development.

12. What steps can I take to be more confident when pointing out these developmental connections to parents? colleagues? naysayers?

13. What is one thing I can do Monday to begin making more time each day to play?

✦ NOTABLE AND QUOTABLE

Play is the most useful tool for preparing children for the future and its tasks.

—Bruno Bettelheim, "The Importance of Play"

*Play is frivolous, wandering according to the whims of curiosity and interest. . . . However, to say that play has no inherent goal does not mean that its results cannot **afterward** be put to good purposes beyond motivating enjoyment.*

—Robert and Michèle Root Bernstein, *Sparks of Genius*

It may be more beneficial that a child should follow energetically some pursuit, of however trifling a nature, and thus acquire perseverance, than that he should be turned from it because of no further advantage to him.

—Charles Darwin

PART 3

CHALLENGES WE FACE

17

Challenges We Face

MY ORIGINAL REASONS for writing this book were various. First, I wanted to provide a sense of affirmation, a pat on the back if you will. Why? Because most of you are already doing these Seven Things! I wanted to show that when we stick to our guns—let kids be kids and provide developmentally appropriate activities—they are going to be just fine! I want you to be able to say to yourself, "YAY ME! Because I am an advocate of playful learning, the children I work with are going to do just fine in school!" That being said, I wanted to expand on the reasons why the Seven Things—whether you've come to do them naturally or not—need to be a part of your child's daily experience, whether they be infants, toddlers, preschoolers, school-aged students, middle-school students, or college-bound seniors. *It is never too late to increase the time we spend each day creating, moving, singing, discussing, observing, reading, and playing.*

I think it would do the world a lot of good if we *all* spent more time doing these things! But my focus for this book is to show that when we make the time to do these things with young children, they go to school ready to learn, wanting more, and excited about school.

The Seven Things, of course, is a guide, not a checklist. And, as I've already alluded to, if you're grounded in developmentally appropriate practice, you are already doing these things, and they are all happening all day long! Please do not feel compelled to design a new schedule!

8:00 a.m. CREATE!

9:00 a.m. MOVE!

10:00 a.m. SING!

11:00 a.m. DISCUSS

Take comfort in the fact you are contributing to a strong foundation by making time each day to do these Seven Things. Notice a few gaps? Maybe an area that needs some bolstering up? No worries, just start salt and peppering your day with a few of the suggested activities I have written about throughout the book. Remember the power of baby steps. It is hard to incorporate new things. Most folks aren't too keen on change. Be patient and gentle with yourself, your colleagues, your classroom, and your family. There will be obstacles. I have provided a brief outline of the major challenges we face when attempting to implement the Seven Things. Perhaps you might be able to identify an area where a specific talent, passion, or ability of yours might assist in facilitating change.

CHALLENGES TO CREATING

* ✫ Creating is often limited to the visual arts, and other forms of creativity are not offered, noticed, or encouraged.
* ✫ There is often no money for basic supplies, such as paper, paint, crayons, and markers.
* ✫ Lip service is paid to the importance of creativity via the implementation of arts-based academic standards.
* ✫ We allow Creativity Killers.
* ✫ Laminated Ladies are still teaching.

CHallenGes to MovinG

* Recess is being eliminated.

* Use of screen-based technology takes the place of moving.

* Physical education requirements are not being fulfilled because of claims that the time is needed for more rigorous academic instruction.

* Equipment is being removed from neighborhood playgrounds due to unnecessary (and often nonexistent) lawsuits.

* Some believe the myth that outside time is wasted time.

* Busy schedules interfere with informal outside playtime.

CHallenGes to sinGinG

* Music is seen as an extracurricular "frill"; thus it is usually the first program to be cut.

* We leave the singing up to professionally recorded songs and forget the power of our own voices.

* We have forgotten the words to songs we sang as children.

* We think we can't sing.

* We aren't aware of Howard Gardner's work on the importance (and long-lasting impact) of musical intelligence.

CHallenGes to DiscussinG

* We do not make time to have conversations with children.

* We allow Discussion Destroyers.

* The emphasis has flipped from one on problem solving, communication, and social skills to a more rigid academic agenda with an emphasis on literacy, mathematics, testing, and the regurgitation of facts.

- ☆ Screen-based technologies often replace human-to-human conversations.

- ☆ We talk *at* children instead of talking *with* them.

- ☆ We are impatient at the length of time it sometimes takes children to express themselves.

CHALLENGES TO OBSERVING

- ☆ We look but do not see.

- ☆ We hear but do not listen.

- ☆ Liability issues and fears of lawsuits force schools to impose "no touching" rules despite the fact we know that humans need physical contact with each other.

- ☆ Sensory experiences are seen as messy activities with no real cognitive purpose or intellectual benefit.

- ☆ Children are served hurried meals of prepackaged convenience foods.

- ☆ Schools and child care environments reek of cleaning products instead of coffee, vanilla, or cinnamon.

CHALLENGES TO READING

- ☆ School libraries are turning into computer labs.

- ☆ There is no money for new books.

- ☆ Librarians are being replaced with technology experts.

- ☆ Videos and computers are becoming the storytellers.

- ☆ Children aren't seeing grown-ups engaged in reading books.

- ☆ Children are not being read to.

CHALLENGES TO PLAYING

* We do not have time for play, because of pressure to do "academic" activities. Some don't understand the real value of play.

* Children playing look like they aren't "doing anything."

* We have forgotten what it was like to play.

* There is a lack of awareness of the power that play has on the social, emotional, spiritual, cognitive, and physical development of our children.

* We feel the need to "defend" play instead of implementing it.

18

Final Thoughts

AS LONG AS we insist on building houses before there are foundations, the houses will continue to crumble and collapse. Yet instead of stepping back and saying, "Hmmm, why do all these houses keep falling down?" we tend to push children harder, starting everything younger, and preparing for everything earlier while thinking, "Oh no, they weren't prepared! They weren't ready! They need something *more*!" when really that is the complete opposite of what they need! We mistakenly think they need something more, when really they just need something else.

Why do we continue to push? Are we worried that if they don't start learning now they will never want to? Do we worry they will want to "play" forever, thus never obtain success? Never go to college? Never get a "good" job? I have met parents who have said if their child doesn't get into X-Y-Z Preschool they will never get into Z-Y-X College. This is insane! It is sad that parents have been somehow trained to think this way. Even more disheartening? Many believe such claims to be true.

When the foundation is strong, we can begin to build the house! In fact, building the house is the next logical step! We make a mistake when we approach "learning" as something we think children would want to avoid. The exact opposite is true. Children are innately curious about the world around them and want to know how it works. The child care center I owned was philosophically grounded in DAP, the Seven Things, and playful learning. Many children stayed with us from the time they were infants until they moved on to kindergarten. Now, I'm being overly general here, but permit me as I make my point. I could walk into the pre-K room and identify INSTANTLY who the "new kids" were as opposed to the children who had grown up with us. How? For the most part, all the new children were up to their eyeballs in cornstarch, glue, playdough, and easel paint, while the children who had spent their childhoods with us were reading to each other, dictating stories, and asking the teachers how to spell certain words. Why? Were they gifted? Of course not. In essence, they'd been given ample time to *do* all of that other stuff. They still could and would, but they didn't *need* it the way the new kids, who had not yet had enough of it, did. The "old timers" had been given time each day to create, move, sing, discuss, observe, read, and play, so their foundations were strong. And when foundations are strong, we can begin building. I don't care how old they are. I cannot stress enough the importance of knowing the difference between building the house because the foundation is strong and building a house because we are caving in to the pressure of "going to kindergarten in the fall." There is a *huge* difference.

Remember my group of fours and fives from earlier in the book who said, "Teach us to read!"? Wanting to read and write and to learn other academic subjects comes naturally when the process is allowed to unfold on its own, but *not when it is forced and pushed*. We must be mindful of our personal agendas, our egos, and our impatience. And while there is nothing wrong with expecting big, huge, academic mansions, there is a lot wrong with selfish, shortsighted demands for big houses when we have neglected the foundations that will hold them up.

We must step back, take a deep breath, and take a good look at what is happening. Only then can we begin to assess the situation in front of us and begin to change how things are being done. I am confident that this can happen. Visit schools, and watch what is happening in them. Many parents say that their preschool is excellent, but it is the upper grades they are worried about. So go hang out there! Meet the teachers at the school your child will be attending. Get to know them. Talk with friends, family, and parents about educational issues. Many times people think "it's not my problem," but it is. Until the administrators and politicians know that you don't like what is happening, it will continue!

I am asked all the time, "Do you testify to the elected officials on behalf of the children and the schools?" Sure. But I'll be honest with you, I can rant and rave and share story after story after story, but the bottom line is that *we put them in those positions!* We must get better at taking our power back. If you don't like what's happening, do something about it! Write a letter to your elected officials and get five of your friends to write one with you, know the issues specifically related to education at election time, and find out where the candidates stand. Meet your child's principal, invite administrators to your informal gatherings, put your child in a school that reflects your belief system, hang out in the classrooms more, homeschool, start a co-op.

Be the change you want to see in the world.

Start small, take baby steps. Talk to a few parents and a few teachers. Let people know this is something you believe in and become vocal. Many are not involved in their child's education. I don't see how you can afford not to be. Many simply send their kids off to the neighborhood school and figure the rest is up to the teachers and staff. You must make a conscious choice to be involved. And by involved I mean *involved*, not just being willing to bake cookies for a holiday party. I mean, for example, do you know if your child gets recess? When do they sing? What about art? How long is the lunch break? Are they outside at lunch, enjoying the break, eating, and chatting with friends and then running around to blow off some steam? Or are they required to eat at their desks, a "working lunch," like little executives? What curriculum do they follow? What is the reading program? What is done when children need extra help? What is done when a child needs more challenges? Are they handled *individually* or forced to stay with the pack, thus not receiving what they need? At what grade does the testing frenzy begin? What engaging projects will now *stop* because they are "not on the test"? Do the teachers have a basic understanding of learning styles, brain development, and the ways in which children learn? Are they familiar with Howard Gardner's theory of multiple intelligences, and do they then use this information to make the classroom engaging for *all* students? Or are we focused on the three Rs and the rest be damned?

When you begin to get involved, you will find your tribe and your circle of support will grow. Then these are the folks you call upon to change the schools and ensure that all children are being given time each day to create, move, sing, discuss, observe, read, and play. Together we will overcome the challenges and will demand places where success is no longer measured by grades, test scores, and exit exams. Instead, it will be measured by the thought behind their questions, the wonder on their faces, the curiosity in their spirit, the persistence in their investigations, and imaginative, innovative suggestions. We will have children who are fun to be around and who can be serious when it is required of them. These children are compassionate and loving. They know how to solve problems (get their shovel back), they appreciate books, songs, and stories, and they are moved by beauty. Children who have been in environments that celebrate discovery and wonder become adults who do the same. But they are not yet adults. They are children. They are our responsibility. We become the guardians of inquiry.

It is said that education is not the filling of a bucket but rather the lighting of a fire. It is our job to keep that fire burning and to keep the flame alive. Use that fire and passion to create that strong foundation. Frame it, pour it, and allow it to set. Some will set faster than others. Some will take awhile, a long while. It can be hard to be patient while your neighbor is building a house and you are still waiting for your cement to dry. Your neighbor, mother-in-law, local politician, testing service agent, and school board president all want to know why you don't have your house started yet. "Look at *our* houses!" they say.

So you look, and you get worried. You look at their big houses and then back at your wet mound of cement. Yet what they don't *say*, and what you don't see, is that in the dark of night, when no one was watching, they began building that house while the cement was still damp. Some never even laid the foundation down but rather built a house in haste to impress the neighbors. "Why bother," they thought, "no one will know, and besides, I want my house up first!"

They are sacrificing their child's experience in the name of their own egos. They want to "win" at whatever the game is they think they are playing.

And while they might appear to be ahead of the game right now, guess what will happen in a year . . . or two . . . or five? Their house will fall down.

"But, damn it!" you say! "My cement is just sitting there! It's not doing anything! And now, oh look! Now the frame is cracking! We are going to be here forever!"

Not forever—but for however long it takes.

Be patient. What does the cement need? A new frame? Provide it. Time? Provide it. More dry to offset the wet? Provide it. To be spread out again within the new frame? Provide it.

Granted you might wait, but in the long run who is benefiting the most? What is an extra six months? Eight months? Year? We're talking about the foundation that will be supporting them for the rest of their life! Why do we feel the need to hurry that up? We owe it to them to make it as strong as possible! Don't rush it. Don't hurry.

Stop now and take a deep breath . . . inhale and exhale.

You will need to be focused, strong, articulate, and brave. But you can do it. Together, we can work to make it better. I share with you; you share with me. I support you; you support me. You support a friend; she supports her colleague. He supports the teachers, and she supports the parent. I express my passion with you, and you tell me of yours. I share with you the fire in my belly, and you take some and use it to light your candle. Then you share your light with someone who then shares with someone else. A candle loses none of its light by lighting another candle. Together we can make the world a little bit better and a little bit brighter.

But that's enough for today, let's get busy.

We got this.
All my best,

Lisa Murphy

BIBLIOGRAPHY

Ackerman, Diane. *A Natural History of the Senses*. New York: Random House, 1990.

American Psychiatric Association. *Diagnostic and Statistical Manual of Mental Disorders*. 4th ed. Washington, DC: American Psychiatric Association, 2000.

———. *Diagnostic and Statistical Manual of Mental Disorders*. 5th ed. Washington, DC: American Psychiatric Association, 2013.

Armstrong, Alison, and Charles Casement. *The Child and the Machine: How Computers Put Our Children's Education at Risk*. Beltsville, MD: Robins Lane Press, 2000.

Armstrong, Thomas. *In Their Own Way*. Jeremy P. Tarcher/Putnam: New York, 2000.

———. *7 Kinds of Smart*. New York: Plume Penguin, 1999.

———. *The Myth of the A.D.D. Child*. New York: Plume Penguin, 1995.

Ashton-Warner, Sylvia. *Teacher*. New York: Simon & Schuster, 1963.

Barbour, Nita H., and Carol Seefeldt. *Developmental Continuity across Preschool and Primary Grades*. Wheaton, MD: Association for Childhood Education International, 1993.

Butler, Dorothy, and Marie Clay. *Reading Begins at Home: Preparing Children for Reading Before They Go to School*. Exeter, NH: Heinemann Educational Books, 1982.

Clemens, Sydney Gurewitz. *The Sun's Not Broken, a Cloud's Just in the Way: On Child-Centered Teaching*. Mt. Ranier, MD: Gryphon House, 1983.

Copple, Carol, and Sue Bredekamp. *Developmentally Appropriate Practice in Early Childhood Programs Serving Children from Birth through Age 8*. 3rd. ed. Washington, DC: National Association for the Education of Young Children, 2009.

Dennison, Paul E. *Brain Gym, Teachers Edition*. Ventura, CA: Edu-Kinesthetics, 1989.

Dimidjian, Victoria Jean, ed. *Play's Place in Public Education for Young Children*. Washington, DC: National Education Association, 1992.

Elkind, David. *Miseducation: Preschoolers at Risk*. New York: Alfred Knopf, 1989.

Fox, Mem. *Dear Mem Fox, I Have Read All Your Books Even the Pathetic Ones*. San Diego: Harcourt Brace Jovanovich, 1992.

Gardner, Howard. *The Unschooled Mind*. New York: Basic Books, 1991.

——. *The Disciplined Mind*. New York: Penguin, 2000.

Goldman, H. H. *Review of General Psychiatry*, 2nd ed. San Mateo, CA: Appleton and Lange, 1988.

Goleman, Daniel, Paul Kaufman, and Michael Ray. *The Creative Spirit*. New York: Dutton, 1992.

Greenberg, Marvin. *Your Children Need Music: A Guide for Parents and Teachers of Young Children*. Englewood Cliffs, NJ: Prentice Hall, 1979.

Hannaford, Carla. *Smart Moves: Why Learning Is Not All in Your Head*. Arlington, VA: Great Ocean Publishers, 1995.

Healy, Jane. *Endangered Minds: Why Our Children Don't Think*. New York: Simon & Schuster, 1990.

——. *How to Have Intelligent and Creative Conversations with Your Kids*. New York: Doubleday, 1992.

Kauffman Early Education Exchange. *Set for Success: Building a Strong Foundation for School Readiness Based on the Social-Emotional Development of Young Children*. Kansas City, MO: Ewing Marion Kauffman Foundation, 2002.

Kellogg, Rhoda. *Analyzing Children's Art*. Palo Alto, CA: National Press Books, 1969.

Kotulak, Ronald. "A Good Beginning: Sending America's Children to School with the Social and Emotional Competence They Need to Succeed," *Chicago Tribune*, 6 September 2000.

Medina, John. *Brain Rules: 12 Principles of Surviving and Thriving at Work, Home, and School*. Seattle: Pear Press, 2008.

Mooney, Carol Garhart. *Swinging Pendulums: Cautionary Tales for Early Childhood Education*. St. Paul, MN: Redleaf Press, 2012.

Murphy, Lisa. *The Ooey Gooey® Handbook: Identifying and Creating Child-Centered Environments*. St. Paul, MN: Redleaf Press, 2001.

——. *Ooey Gooey® Tooey: 140 Exciting Hands-On Activity Ideas for Young Children*. St. Paul, MN: Redleaf Press, 2009.

Quindlen, Anna. "The Days of Guilded Rigatoni." *New York Times*, 12 May 1991.

Rivkin, Mary. *The Great Outdoors: Restoring Children's Right to Play Outside*. Washington, DC: National Association for the Education of Young Children, 1995.

Root-Bernstein, Robert, and Michèle Root-Bernstein. *Sparks of Genius: Thirteen Thinking Tools of the World's Most Creative People*. Boston: Houghton Mifflin, 1999.

von Oech, Roger. *A Whack on the Side of the Head: How You Can Be More Creative*. New York: Grand Central Publishing, 2008.

SUGGESTED READINGS

Here is a short list of selected favorites from my personal bookshelf.

Ayers, William. *To Teach: The Journey of a Teacher.* 1st and 2nd eds. New York: Teachers College Press, 1994, 2001.

Bettelheim, Bruno. "The Importance of Play," *Atlantic Monthly,* March 1987.

Bos, Bev, and Jenny Chapman. *Tumbling over the Edge: A Rant for Children's Play.* Roseville, CA: Turn the Page Press, 2005.

Bronson, Po, and Ashley Merryman. *NurtureShock: New Thinking about Children.* New York: Twelve, 2009.

Brown, Stuart, and Christopher Vaughan. *Play: How It Shapes the Brain, Opens the Imagination, and Invigorates the Soul.* New York: Avery, 2009.

Carlson, Frances. *Big Body Play: Why Boisterous, Vigorous, and Very Physical Play Is Essential to Children's Development and Learning.* Washington, DC: National Association for the Education of Young Children, 2011.

Carlsson-Paige, Nancy. *Taking Back Childhood: Helping Your Kids Thrive in a Fast-Paced, Media-Saturated, Violence-Filled World.* New York: Plume, 2009.

Chenfeld, Mimi Brodsky. *Teaching in the Key of Life: A Collection of the Writings of Mimi Brodsky Chenfeld.* Washington, DC: National Association for the Education of Young Children, 1993.

Crain, William. *Reclaiming Childhood: Letting Children Be Children in Our Achievement-Oriented Society.* New York: Times Books, 2003.

Curtis, Deb, and Margie Carter. *The Art of Awareness: How Observation Can Transform Your Teaching.* St. Paul, MN: Redleaf Press, 2013.

———. *Designs for Living and Learning: Transforming Early Childhood Environments.* St. Paul, MN: Redleaf Press, 2015.

Dewey, John. *Experience and Education.* New York: Collier Books, 1938.

Diamond, Marion. *Magic Trees of the Mind.* New York: Plume, 1999.

Elkind, David. *The Power of Play: Learning What Comes Naturally.* Cambridge: Da Capo Press, 2007.

Fox, Mem. *Radical Reflections: Passionate Opinions on Teaching, Learning, and Living.* San Diego: Harcourt Brace & Co., 1993.

———. *Reading Magic: Why Reading Aloud to Our Children Will Change Their Lives Forever.* New York: Harcourt, 2001.

Frost, Joe, et al. *The Developmental Benefits of Playgrounds.* Olney, MD: Association for Childhood Education International, 2004.

Galinsky, Ellen. *Mind in the Making: The Seven Essential Life Skills Every Child Needs.* New York: William Morrow, 2010.

Goffin, Stacie, and Valora Washington. *Ready or Not: Leadership Choices in Early Care and Education.* New York: Teachers College Press, 2007.

Gonzales-Mena, Janet. *Dragon Mom: Confessions of a Child-Development Expert.* Napa, CA: Rattle OK Publications, 1995.

Gopnik, Alison, et al. *The Scientist in the Crib: What Early Learning Tells Us about The Mind.* New York: Perennial, 2001.

Gray, Peter. *Free to Learn: Why Unleashing the Instinct to Play Will Make Our Children Happier, More Self-Reliant, and Better Students for Life.* New York: Basic Books, 2013.

Hainstock, Elizabeth. *The Essential Montessori.* Plume: New York, 1986.

Healy, Jane. *Failure to Connect: How Computers Affect Our Children's Minds—for Better and Worse.* Simon & Schuster: New York, 1998.

———. *Different Learners: Identifying, Preventing, and Treating Your Child's Learning Problems.* New York: Simon & Schuster, 2010.

Hern, Matt, ed. *Deschooling Our Lives.* Philadelphia: New Society, 1996.

Hirsh-Pasek, Kathy, and Roberta Golinkoff, with Diane Eyer. *Einstein Never Used Flash Cards: How Our Children Really Learn—and Why They Need to Play More and Memorize Less.* Emmaus, PA: Rodale, 2003.

Hirsh-Pasek, Kathy, et al. *A Mandate for Playful Learning in Preschool: Presenting the Evidence.* New York: Oxford University Press, 2009.

Hodgins, Daniel. *Boys: Changing the Classroom, Not the Child.* Manchester, MI: Wilderness Adventure Books, 2009.

Jenkinson, Sally. *The Genius of Play: Celebrating the Spirit of Childhood.* Stroud, UK: Hawthorn Press, 2001.

Johnson, Jeff, and Denita Dinger. *Let Them Play: An Early Learning (Un) Curriculum.* St. Paul, MN: Redleaf Press, 2012.

Jones, Elizabeth and John Nimmo. *Emergent Curriculum*. Washington, DC: National Association for the Education of Young Children, 1994.

Kohn, Alfie. *Punished by Rewards: The Trouble with Gold Stars, Incentive Plans, A's, and Other Bribes*. Boston: Houghton Mifflin, 1993.

———. *The Schools Our Children Deserve: Moving beyond Traditional Classrooms and "Tougher Standards."* Boston: Houghton Mifflin, 1999.

———. *What to Look for in a Classroom . . . and Other Essays*. San Francisco: Jossey-Bass, 1998.

———. *The Case against Standardized Testing: Raising the Scores, Ruining the Schools*. Portsmouth, NH: Heinemann, 2000.

Linn, Susan. *The Case for Make Believe: Saving Play in a Commercialized World*. New York: New Press, 2008.

Louv, Richard. *The Nature Principle: Human Restoration and the End of Nature-Deficit Disorder*. Chapel Hill, NC: Algonquin Books, 2011.

———. *Last Child in the Woods: Saving Our Children from Nature-Deficit Disorder*. Chapel Hill, NC: Algonquin Books, 2005.

Mander, Jerry. *Four Arguments For the Elimination of Television*. New York: Quill, 1978.

Máté, Ferenc. *A Reasonable Life: Toward a Simpler, Secure, More Humane Existence*. New York: Albatross Publishing, 1993.

Mogel, Wendy. *The Blessing of a Skinned Knee: Using Jewish Teachings to Raise Self-Reliant Children*. New York: Scribner, 2001.

Montessori, Maria. *The Absorbent Mind*. New York: Henry Holt, 1995.

Mooney, Carol Garhart. *Theories of Childhood: Dewey, Montessori, Erikson, Piaget and Vygotsky*. St. Paul, MN: Redleaf Press, 2000.

Nabhan, Gary Paul. *The Geography of Childhood: Why Children Need Wild Places*. Boston: Beacon Press, 1994.

Newkirk, Thomas, *Misreading Masculinity: Boys, Literacy, and Popular Culture*. Portsmouth, NH: Heinemann, 2002.

Ohanian, Susan. *What Happened to Recess and Why Are Our Children Struggling in Kindergarten?* McGraw Hill: New York, 2002.

Paley, Vivian Gussin. *You Can't Say You Can't Play*. Cambridge, MA: Harvard University Press, 1992.

———. *A Child's Work: The Importance of Fantasy Play*. Chicago: University of Chicago Press, 2004.

Pearce, Joseph Chilton. *Evolution's End: Claiming the Potential of Our Intelligence*. San Francisco: Harper, 1992.

Postman, Neil. *The End of Education*. New York: Vintage Books, 1996.

Sanders, Barry. *A Is for Ox: Violence, Electronic Media, and the Silencing of the Written Word*. New York: Vintage Books, 1994.

Shonkoff, Jack, and Deborah Phillips, eds. *From Neurons to Neighborhoods: The Science of Early Child Development*. Washington, DC: National Academy Press, 2000.

Shumaker, Heather. *It's OK Not to Share and Other Renegade Rules for Raising Competent and Compassionate Kids*. New York: Penguin, 2012.

Singer, Dorothy, Roberta Michnick Golinkoff, and Kathy Hirsh-Pasek. *Play = Learning: How Play Motivates and Enhances Children's Cognitive and Social-Emotional Growth*. New York: Oxford University Press, 2006.

Skenazy, Lenore. *Free-Range Kids: Giving Our Children the Freedom We Had without Going Nuts with Worry*. San Francisco: Jossey-Bass, 2009.

Stoll, Clifford. *High-Tech Heretic: Why Computers Don't Belong in the Classroom and Other Reflections by a Computer Contrarian*. New York: Doubleday, 1999.

Taylor Gatto, John. *Dumbing Us Down*. Philadelphia: New Society, 1992.

Topal, Cathy Weisman, and Lella Gandini. *Beautiful Stuff! Learning with Found Materials*. Worcester, MA: Davis Publications, 1999.

Tulley, Gever Carson. *Fifty Dangerous Things You Should Let Your Children Do*. New York: New American Library, 2011.

Zigler, Edward, Dorothy G. Singer, and Sandra J. Bishop-Josef, eds. *Children's Play: The Roots of Reading*. Washington, DC: Zero to Three Press, 2004